THE MONOPOLY® OMNIBUS

THE MONOPOLY® OMNIBUS

GYLES BRANDRETH

Willow Books
Collins
8 Grafton Street, London W1
1985

Willow Books
William Collins Sons & Co Ltd
London · Glasgow · Sydney
Auckland · Toronto · Johannesburg

First published in Great Britain 1985
© Gyles Brandreth 1985

Designed by Clive Sutherland

ISBN 0 00 218166 5

Filmset by Rowland Phototypesetting Ltd,
Bury St Edmunds, Suffolk

Printed in Great Britain by
Billings & Sons, Worcester

CONTENTS

CONTENTS

ACKNOWLEDGEMENTS

This book would not have been possible without the generous cooperation of Waddingtons Games in the UK and Parker Brothers in the USA.

For their unstinting help I am especially indebted to Victor Watson and Beric Watson, who as young boys played Monopoly in Britain in 1935 and who are now, respectively, Chairman of John Waddington plc and Managing Director of Waddingtons Games Ltd. Their assistance has been invaluable, though blame for any sins of omission or commission must be laid at my door, not theirs.

In 1974, as official European Monopoly Champion, I had the pleasure of visiting the headquarters of Parker Brothers, in Salem, Massachusetts, where President Randolph Barton generously allowed me to dip into the remarkable Monopoly archives.

I must also acknowledge the invaluable assistance of Douglas Brearley, John Watson, Sue Ruszczynski, David Dawson, Andrew McKeon and Michael Curl.

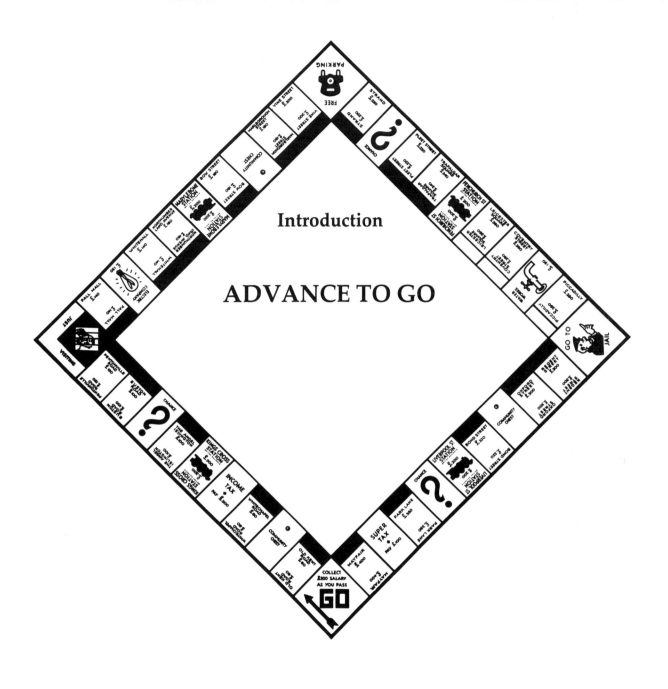

Introduction

ADVANCE TO GO

I owe my life to Monopoly.

That may seem an extravagant claim, but it's true. It was over a Monopoly board that my parents first met and fell in love.

Back in the winter of 1936 my father, a young lawyer just starting out on his career and newly arrived in London, bought one of the first Monopoly sets to be sold in Britain. He took the game back to his lodgings and asked the landlady if she wanted to try it out with him. She said she felt she was too old for board games,* but suggested my father might like to approach the Canadian lady and her daughter who had just moved into rooms on the top floor. He'd never met them, knew nothing about them, but with a spring in his stride and the Monopoly board under his arm, he climbed the stairs to play the game and meet his future wife.

Forty years later, when that Monopoly tyro and the Canadian lady's daughter were celebrating their ruby wedding anniversary, I was in New York as the official European Monopoly Champion doing my best to uphold the family honour by coming third in the World Monopoly Championships. Who knows, had I written this book at the time I might even have come first.

We have been games fanatics in my family for generations. A century ago, my great-great-grandfather, a New York Senator in his day, published *Brandreth's Puzzle Book*, a compendium of his favourite games, pastimes and brain-teasers. The book was intended to promote the sale of

---

* To be a London landlady and know so little about life is strange, but there we are. You can be too *young* for board games, but never too old.

> 'With their simple and unequivocal rules, games are like so many islands of order in the vague untidy chaos of experience. In games one passes from the incomprehensible universe of given reality into a neat little man-made world where everything is clear, purposive and easy to understand.'
>
> *Aldous Huxley*

Brandreth's Pills – 'a medicine that acts directly on the stomach, bowels and liver, and through them purifies the blood: they cure rheumatism, headache, biliousness, constipation, dyspepsia and liver complaint' – but having been to Sing Sing, the bizarre location of the Brandreth Pill Factory, and both tasted the medicine and read the book, I'm inclined to think my ancestors were better gamesmen than they were pharmacists.

Of course, we Brandreths are games inventors as well as players, but alas for us we've never been in the same league as the Darrows. I always thought (as so many do) that it was Clarence Darrow, lawyer, lecturer and prophet,* who invented Monopoly. In fact it was *Charles* Darrow.

When an unemployed salesman, at the height of the Depression, sat down at his kitchen table and sketched out a board game based on the street names of an East Coast American seaside resort, little did he know he would be starting a 'leisure revolution'. The unemployed salesman was Charles Darrow, and the full complex story of the genesis of Monopoly will be told in Part One (page 17). Suffice it for now to say that Charles Darrow was without doubt the most successful games designer who ever lived. Monopoly made Charles Darrow a millionaire.

That, of course, is the thrill of Monopoly. When you play it, you too can become a millionaire – not perhaps for a lifetime, but at least for an evening. What's more you can become a millionaire at your friends' expense, without doing them any lasting damage and without running any real risks

---

* It was Clarence Darrow (1857–1938) who said, 'When I was a boy I was told that anyone could become President; I'm beginning to believe it.'

> 'Man only plays when in the full meaning of the word he is a man, and he is only completely a man when he plays.'
> *Friedrich von Schiller*

yourself. Monopoly is the surest, safest, fastest way to a fortune – if you can win, that is. And you *can* win if you're determined to, because Monopoly isn't just a game of chance.

Nor is Monopoly just a chance to play a game. It's also an opportunity to learn a few things about life and how to survive in the jungle of the real world as well as in that make-believe world where you can buy Park Lane for £350. That's why, in the pages that follow, alongside the rules of the game and the tips on tactics and strategy, I've been bold enough to include some of the axioms and maxims and laws* that I believe can apply as much to Life as to Monopoly.

And I want you to know that if you're one of those who feel that to spend hour upon hour playing a mere board game at a time of national and international crisis is tantamount to rearranging the deck chairs on board the Titanic, you're not alone – but you are wrong. Of all the amazing things I've learnt in my thirty-seven years – among them the fact that you can cook a dozen omelettes with one ostrich egg, that Jayne Mansfield and Marie Antoinette had identical bust measurements, that happiness can't buy money, that Winston Churchill and Aristotle Onassis were regular Monopoly players – perhaps the most remarkable is that, for our psychological well-being, we need, yes, we really do *need* to play games . . . and I reckon Monopoly's one of the games we need to play most.

GYLES BRANDRETH

---

* Sadly I found no place for my favourite: Cole's Law (sliced raw cabbage).

Part One

THE STORY OF
MONOPOLY

THE STORY OF MONOPOLY

The year was 1930. The place, Germantown, Pennsylvania. Charles Darrow, like several million other Americans, was a victim of the Depression. An out-of-work salesman of heating and engineering equipment, he was a resourceful and determined individual who managed to support himself and his family by taking on odd jobs whenever he could get them. He'd do anything – home decorating, mending old irons, mowing lawns, walking dogs – but in the time he had to spare (and there was plenty of that) he liked to invent things. His early inventions included a bat and ball game and a simplified bridge scoring pad, but he had no commercial success with them.

Unemployment, of course, was almost universal and many of Darrow's friends were in the same position as he was. Going out for entertainment, to a film or the theatre, was a financial impossibility and the notion of a television in every home was still a science fiction fantasy, so Darrow and his circle would spend their evenings in one another's houses, talking or playing cards or playing board games.

Darrow wanted to invent a new board game, not only so he could play it with his friends, but also because he hoped that he might be able to make some money with it. Why he chose to devise a game based on real estate nobody knows. In later years he couldn't remember. In 1924 a property game called The Landlord's Game had been patented by Elizabeth Magie (later Phillips) of Virginia. This game, devised as propaganda for a theory of taxation (the 'single tax' theory expounded by Henry George), involved trips round a playing board with the purchase of property and the charging of rents. Other similarities to Monopoly are that both games have nine spaces between the corners, both have

THE STORY OF MONOPOLY

'Go to Jail' corners, Railways, the Electric Company and Waterworks, and a bonus when passing GO. Darrow must almost certainly have played The Landlord's Game or at least have been familiar with it. But the special feature of Monopoly, that sets of property must be acquired before houses or hotels can be built, was entirely original, and it is this feature, above all others, which has made Monopoly the best of all property trading board games. Certainly, also, the design of Darrow's board, and the names of the streets on it, were inspired by his own happy memories of the vacations he and his wife took in Atlantic City in the 'good old days' before the Depression.

The materials needed for the prototype Monopoly set were all close at hand. For the board he used a piece of oilcloth that had been a table covering. The houses and hotels he made from scraps of wooden moulding. The cards and Title Deeds were all handwritten. It is said that the original tokens were charms from his wife's charm bracelet.

From the games played with this primitive equipment word began to get round that Monopoly was 'quite some board game'. Within months people in the neighbourhood were asking Darrow for sets of their own so they could play the game themselves at home. As demand grew, Darrow found that he was unable to cope with it, so he contracted out the board production to a friend who was a jobbing printer. In this way he managed to increase his daily output to six sets, which he sold for $2.50 a set. But the demand for the game continued to grow and soon Darrow had to contract out the complete printing and packaging.

As well as selling to friends, acquaintances and neighbours, Darrow also sold some sets to department stores

THE STORY OF MONOPOLY

in Philadelphia – the John Wanamaker department store in Philadelphia was the first to put the game on sale, in 1934. With orders arriving in wholesale quantities, eventually the time came when Darrow realized he had to make a crucial decision: either to raise some capital himself and go into manufacturing and marketing Monopoly in a big way, or to sell the concept to an existing games manufacturer in return for a royalty payment on all sets sold.

Unwilling to take the financial risk himself, he approached Parker Brothers some time in 1934. Parker Brothers, then, as now, were the world's largest games manufacturers. Edward P. Parker, who later became president of the company, had this to say about Mr Darrow's visit:

'After Darrow left, the executives played the game several times and, although we personally enjoyed it, everyone felt it could never be a popular success. It violated several of what we thought were elementary rules for a family game. We always felt that forty-five minutes was about the right length of time for a game, but Monopoly could go on for hours. Also, a game was supposed to have a definite end somewhere. In Monopoly you kept going around and around. The rules involving mortgages and rents seemed much too complicated. The decision to turn it down was unanimous.'

Parker Brothers rejected the game, telling Charles Darrow that there were 'fifty-two fundamental errors' in the design of the game. Darrow was disappointed by the rejection, angered even, but far from despairing. By Christmas 1934 he was working fourteen hours a day to keep up with orders. He had 5000 Monopoly sets made up for the Christmas

THE STORY OF
MONOPOLY

season, and he sold them all – bringing his total sales for the year to 20 000.

By now the game was being distributed to stores in New York as well as Philadelphia. One of the people who bought a set from the New York toy shop F. A. O. Schwartz was a close friend of Sally Barton, the daughter of Parker Brothers' founder George Parker and the wife of Parker Brothers' president Robert Barton. She was so captivated by the game that she could not help but pass on her enthusiasm to Sally, who in turn told her father and her husband. By this time, too, Parker Brothers' sales representatives were coming back with ecstatic reports about the game.

So, in 1935, Parker Brothers approached Darrow and offered him an attractive royalty agreement. 'I gladly accepted and have never regretted that decision,' Darrow was to write later. He retired at the age of forty-six on the proceeds brought to him by Monopoly. He became a gentleman farmer in Bucks County, Pennsylvania, developing a keen interest in foreign travel, home movies and the cultivation of rare and exotic orchids – far removed from the struggles and hardships of 1930. He continued to invent games but none had the success of Monopoly. At the age of 78 he died, a multi-millionaire, leaving his heirs a huge fortune in royalties and potential income.

Parker Brothers refined the game, clarified and simplified the rules and launched it nationwide in 1935. It became the biggest thing they had ever undertaken. They were soon producing 20 000 sets a week. As the Christmas season approached, enquiries poured in so thick and fast that they had to use laundry baskets lined up in the corridors to store the unprocessed orders. Within a year they had sold more

THE STORY OF MONOPOLY

than a million sets. Even then they reckoned it was only a passing craze. It couldn't possibly last. In December 1936 they actually made a decision to stop manufacturing the game altogether – but the sheer weight of continuing public demand quickly forced them to change their minds.

Parker Brothers just about coped with the demand for Monopoly in the USA. But for overseas sales they had to resort to the licensed manufacture of the game by others. In the early part of 1935, Parker Brothers sent a sample of Monopoly to Waddingtons in the UK. John Waddington Ltd had started out as printers for the theatre but by that time were branching out into packaging and already had a small playing card division. The company had begun to produce Lexicon the previous year and had sent a sample to Parker Brothers with a view to their manufacturing it in the USA under licence. So it was natural for Parker Brothers to return the compliment with Monopoly.

One Friday night, the head of Waddingtons, Victor Watson senior, handed the set to his son Norman (who was managing the playing card division), saying, 'Look this over and tell me what you think of it.' Norman Watson remembers the event thus:

'I played an imaginary game against myself continuing through Friday night, Saturday night and Sunday night. I was enthralled and captivated. I had never found a game so absorbing, and thus Monopoly was first played in England at my home. I was so enthusiastic that on the Monday morning I persuaded my father to make a telephone call to Parker Brothers. Today transatlantic telephone calls are commonplace, but this was the first one

THE STORY OF MONOPOLY

ever made by Waddingtons and I was told it was the first one ever received by Parker Brothers from Europe, so that, apart from its far-reaching consequences, the call itself was something of a landmark.'

Before putting Monopoly into production, Waddingtons decided that the game would have more appeal in the UK if the original Atlantic City place names were changed. Victor Watson, therefore, asked his secretary, Marjory Phillips, to take a walk around London 'to get the right names', and they then worked together to settle a final list of place names. Thus the British version came to have London landmarks, the railroads became railway stations, the dollars became pounds and the cards were changed accordingly.

Waddingtons have continued to manufacture Monopoly ever since, apart from a brief halt in commercial production during World War II. Even at this time Monopoly played its part. The War Office commissioned Waddingtons to produce games which, if properly used, would help prisoners of war. The company soon realized the significance of the phrase 'if properly used'. A secret department was set up at the company's headquarters, manned by a few of their most trusted staff. The job was to make Monopoly sets into the boards of which were inserted silk maps showing escape routes from the particular prison to which each game was to be sent. Into the other side of the board was inserted a tiny compass and several fine-quality files. The Monopoly money was replaced by money of the country to which the game was to be sent – Germany, Austria or Italy. Thus was given a new twist to the phrase 'Get Out Of Jail Free'.

Over the years Monopoly has changed very little. It was

THE STORY OF MONOPOLY

revamped slightly in 1972. The houses, hotels, the ship and the racing car tokens were redesigned. All the tokens were increased in size by 50 per cent. The dice and Title Deed cards were also enlarged. The money, for the first time, was printed on both sides to make it more like the real thing. But these were all very minor alterations. The board and box remained unchanged.

Monopoly is now manufactured under licence in thirty-two countries, spanning five continents. It has been translated into seventeen languages, including French, Afrikaans, German, Dutch, Swedish, Finnish, Norwegian, Hindi, Greek, Portuguese, Japanese, Chinese, Arabic, and Danish. Versions in different Spanish dialects are used in Colombia, Venezuela and Spain, and there are three versions in Spain itself – Madrid Castilian, Barcelona Castilian and Barcelona Catalan.

In the various overseas versions the property locations are generally changed to indigenous street names and the dollars/pounds changed to the local currency. The original Park Place and Boardwalk on the American board became Park Lane and Mayfair in Britain, and Rue de la Paix and Avenue des Champs Elysées in France. In Spain and Germany they are Paseo de la Castellana and Paseo del Prado, and Parkstrasse and Schlossallee. The Arabic version, manufactured and exported by Waddingtons, uses translations of the London street names, while the Japanese version uses translations of the original Atlantic City street names.

In Cuba Monopoly was very popular until Castro came to power. He ordered all sets to be seized, denouncing it as 'symbolic of an imperialistic system'. It is, however, rumoured that Monopoly is still played there by undercover enthusiasts. It is also suspected that in East Germany, in spite of the fact that Monopoly has been banned for the masses, Communist officials smuggle in sets from the West for their own entertainment – the party bosses, in fact, have a Monopoly monopoly. In the USSR the government has outlawed it as 'a decadent instrument of capitalism'. But, during the 1959 American National Exhibition in Moscow, the six Monopoly sets on display there had all disappeared by the time the exhibition ended.

Interest in Monopoly has become so widespread that national championships have become regular events. Those in Britain started in 1972. Organized by Waddingtons, they have been held in a variety of unusual but appropriate venues – in Fenchurch Street Station, on top of the atomic pile at Oldbury-on-Severn power station ('The Electric Company'), on a train from Liverpool Street station to Kings Cross via Fenchurch Street, and in London's Park Lane Hotel. In the USA to mark Monopoly's fortieth anniversary in 1975, Parker Brothers decided to organize a World Tournament. World Championships have been held every two or three years since then. You will find more details of the national and world championships in Part Four (page 183).

There are a very large number of players who are not content with wheeling and dealing in the comfort of their own living rooms. For some reason, Monopoly fanatics feel compelled to play their game in lifts, in tree-houses, in bathtubs, underground, underwater, even on balance beams. So widespread is this desire that Parker Brothers had to establish a committee to adjudicate on and record

THE STORY OF MONOPOLY

marathon records in the various categories.

Since 1935, Parker Brothers estimate that they have sold over 100 million sets. They have 'built' over 3 billion little green houses, making them by far the biggest property company in the world. The amount of 'money' printed daily by Parker Brothers far exceeds the actual dollar output of the US Treasury. In Britain alone Waddingtons have sold 15 million sets – that's over 480 million houses and nearly £200 000 000 000 in Monopoly money. People seem to like playing Monopoly!

Part Two

HOW TO PLAY

or
'Everything You Always Wanted to
Know about Monopoly But Were
Unable to Discover by
Reading the Rules'

THE AIM OF THE GAME

Monopoly is a trading game for two to six players (although it can be played with more). The aim is to become the richest player – by buying and selling properties, by making your opponents pay rents to you, and by avoiding as far as possible the necessity of paying rents to them.

In the normal full version of the game this aim is achieved by driving all your opponents into bankruptcy. There is no doubt that this is the clearest outcome – and the most satisfying. When all your opponents have been bankrupted and you are the only one who is solvent there is no doubt at all who is the winner!

Runyon's Law

The race is not always to the swift, nor the battle to the strong, but that's the way to bet

THE AIM OF THE GAME
Short Game

When played in the full version a game can last several hours, which is why many people prefer to play a shorter version of the game, as described in the official rules. The game ends at the end of a previously agreed time limit. Then the players cash in all their assets and the richest player is the winner.

The short version of the game may have its merits, but any real enthusiast (particularly one with time on his hands and a killer instinct) will agree that there is nothing to beat the satisfaction of winning a full game by bankrupting all your opponents.

THE AIM OF THE GAME
Chance and Skill

Since the moves of the players are decided by rolling dice, Monopoly is obviously a game of chance. However there is a good deal of scope for offsetting the element of chance by the application of skill and strategy. With a bit of luck this book will succeed in its aim of demonstrating how you can develop the necessary skill and strategy to enable you to win more often.

Herbert's Law of Success

Skill and confidence are an unconquered army

W. C. Fields's Dictum

If at first you don't succeed, try again. Then quit.
No use being a damn fool about it

Historical Note

W. C. Fields played Monopoly – twice

EQUIPMENT
The Board

The Monopoly board consists of a square layout with nine spaces on each side and four corners. The corners are allocated to the GO, JAIL, FREE PARKING and GO TO JAIL spaces. The side spaces consist mainly of Building Sites, grouped into eight different colour groups. Each colour group consists of either two or three properties. The remaining side spaces represent four Railway Stations, two Utilities (the Electric Company and the Water Works), three Chance spaces, three Community Chest spaces, and finally and most disagreeably the INCOME TAX and SUPER TAX spaces.

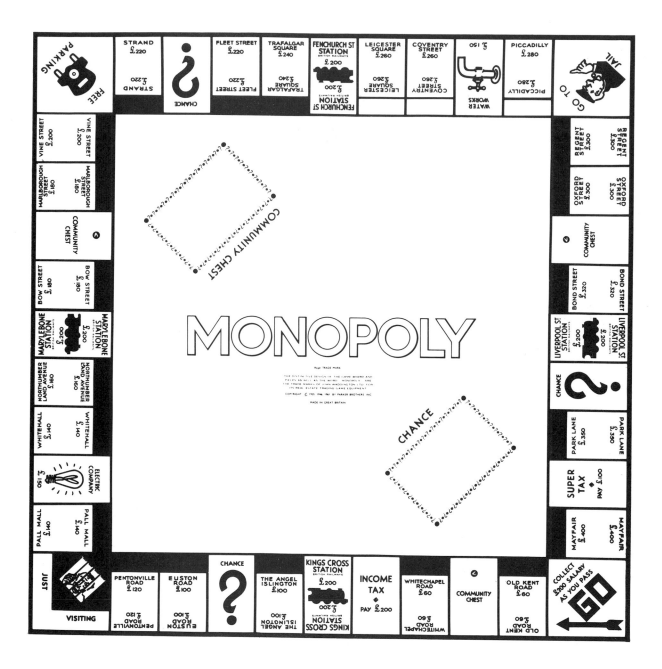

EQUIPMENT
Dice and Tokens

There are two dice, to determine the movements of the players, and tokens of various shapes to represent the players on their travels around the board.

There are 32 houses and 12 hotels, and Title Deeds for each property on the board (including Railway Stations and Utilities). At the beginning of the game all properties and buildings are held by the Bank. The Title Deeds should be displayed so that all players may see which properties are available for purchase.

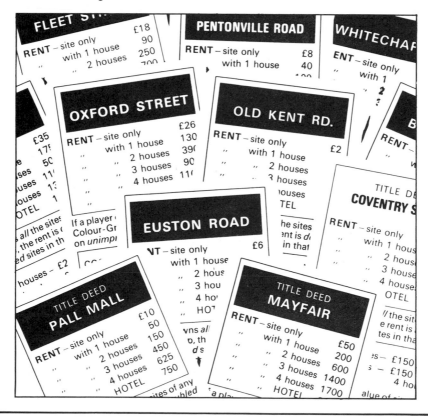

EQUIPMENT
Chance and Community Chest

There is a pack of Chance cards and a pack of Community Chest cards. Each pack should be thoroughly shuffled, at the start of every game, before being placed face down on its designated space near the centre of the board.

CHANCE

YOU HAVE WON A
CROSSWORD COMPETITION
COLLECT £100

COMMUNITY CHEST

PAY YOUR INSURANCE
PREMIUM £50

EQUIPMENT
Cash

Finally there is the cash, consisting of bank notes of various
denominations. At the start of the game each player is given
£1500, divided as follows:
2 £500 bank notes
4 £100 bank notes
1 £50 bank note
1 £20 bank note
2 £10 bank notes
1 £5 bank note
5 £1 bank notes
The remaining cash is held by the Bank.

EQUIPMENT
Playing Area

For Monopoly you need quite a large playing area – for the board, for the Bank to set out its cash and Title Deeds, and for each player to set out his/her cash and Title Deeds.

If you can sustain the Lotus Position for hours on end, play on the floor; if not, use a large table with the board placed centrally so that it is within easy reach of all the players. Just as with any competitive sport, Monopoly has physical hazards comparable to tennis elbow or runner's toe. In medical jargon, 'Monopoly knees' refers to the acute syndrome of sitting cross-legged for long durations.

Aldiss's Rule for Peaceable Play

Keep violence in the mind where it belongs

THE BANK
Choosing the Banker

Before the game begins a Banker must be chosen. Usually one of the players will agree to take on the role of Banker, but if there are more than five players someone may act as full-time Banker and take no other part in the game.

If one player elects to be the Banker, that is fine. If there is more than one player wishing to be the Banker, or if no one is willing to take on the position, then the choice of Banker should be made by throwing the dice. The player throwing the highest total with the dice becomes the Banker.

However the Banker is chosen, it is important that he should be efficient and trustworthy. If he is also taking part in the game as a player it is essential that he should keep his two roles – as Banker and as player – quite separate.

Gross's Law

When two people meet to decide how to spend a third person's money, fraud will result

The Monopoly Corollary

When a player and the Banker are one and the same person, treat them as two and watch out for the fraud

THE BANK
Functions of the Bank

The Bank has to perform the following functions:
(a) It holds all the Title Deed cards and houses and hotels prior to purchase by the players.
(b) It holds all cash not held by the players.
(c) It pays a salary of £200 to each player passing or landing on GO.
(d) It pays bonuses awarded to players by Chance or Community Chest cards.
(e) It collects fines from the players, as determined by Chance or Community Chest cards.
(f) It collects taxes from players landing on the INCOME TAX and SUPER TAX spaces.
(g) When a player lands on an unowned property the Bank either sells the property to that player or puts it up for auction.
(h) It loans money to players, when required, on mortgages. It also collects the mortgage value plus 10 per cent interest when a player wishes to lift a mortgage, and collects a transfer fee of 10 per cent of the mortgage value when a mortgaged property is transferred from one player to another.
(i) It sells houses and hotels to players, and buys them back for one-half the original purchase price. When there is a shortage of buildings available for sale, the Bank may be required to auction off its remaining stock of buildings.

The Monopoly Corollary

When playing Monopoly at the White House, don't let the President be Banker

THE BANK
Shortage of Cash

In normal circumstances the Bank will always have enough cash to carry out its functions. Occasionally, however, in exceptional circumstances – if there are a large number of players or if a game goes on for a longer time than usual – the Bank may find itself in temporary cash-flow difficulties. An important point to note is that the Bank can not become bankrupt – it is assumed to have infinite reserves. So in this situation the Banker should provide him/herself with some blank slips of paper and write on these to create whatever extra cash may be required to keep the game going.

The Banker's Revenge
In matters of dispute, the Bank's balance will always be smaller than yours

THE PLAY
Starting a Game

A Banker has been chosen, the Chance and Community Chest cards have been shuffled and placed on the appropriate spaces, each player has been given £1500 in cash, and each player's token is on GO. You are now ready to start a game.

The Banker throws the two dice, then each of the other players does likewise. The player throwing the highest total with the two dice starts the play.

One situation may occur here which is not covered by the rules. Suppose there are three players – one throws a 4 and a 1 and the other two both roll a 5 and a 3. What do you do in this situation? The fairest solution is for the two players throwing the highest total to throw the dice again, the player with the highest total on the second throw starting the game.

THE PLAY
A Player's Turn

The turn to play always passes to the left. Each player in turn throws the two dice and then moves his token the number of spaces indicated by the total of the two dice. Moves are around the board in the direction of the arrow on the GO space. According to the space a player's token lands on, he may be required or entitled to perform various actions – buy property, pay rent or taxes, draw a Chance or Community Chest card, go to JAIL, etc. His turn is not completed until he has done this (and see the special rules when doubles are thrown, page 46). The dice are then passed to the next player.

A player's token remains on the space occupied at the end of his move, and proceeds from there when his turn to play comes round again.

Why not appoint a 'ombudsman' or official permanent referee who can hold court on disputes for regular family play?

THE PLAY
Timing of Transactions

An issue which has caused countless disagreements over the years is the question of when transactions (such as buying houses or hotels from the Bank, mortgaging property or lifting mortgages, or trading with another player) may be carried out.

The official rules say, 'Undeveloped Sites, Railway Stations and Utilities (but not buildings thereon) may be sold to any player as a private transaction for any amount that the owner can get.' What the rules do not make clear is when such transactions may take place. Can you trade property with player A in the middle of player B's turn?

About selling houses and hotels the rules have this to say, 'Houses and Hotels may be resold by players to the Bank only, but this may be done at any time'. *At any time!* Is this to be taken literally?

If you may sell houses and hotels at any time, what about buying houses and hotels? The rules say that a player may buy *houses* from the Bank 'at any time, in his turn'. *In his turn!* That seems clear enough. But the rules do not specify the same restriction on the buying of *hotels*. It is all rather confusing.

Imagine this situation. You own the complete dark blue property group – Park Lane and Mayfair – and you have erected four houses on each site. It is the turn of one of your opponents; his token is on Regent Street and he has just thrown double 3. You see at a glance that his token is going to land on Park Lane, so you thrust £400 at the Banker and demand two hotels in place of the houses on your dark blue properties. You are in the process of placing a hotel on Park Lane just as your opponent (who is rather slow) places his token there. There is clearly going to be an argument about

THE PLAY
Timing of Transactions

the amount of rent that is payable. Is it £1500 (Park Lane with hotel) or £1300 (Park Lane with four houses)? Or is it £70 for the site only, because the four houses have been removed and the hotel not yet erected? Of course, if this opponent happened to be the Banker there is no way you would have had an opportunity to buy any hotels in the first place!

Obviously the situation described here is absurd, unfair, undignified and unworkable. To avoid this kind of confusion the following rules are normally adhered to:

1   You may buy and sell buildings, mortgage property or lift mortgages at any time *during your own turn*.
2   You may buy and sell buildings, mortgage property or lift mortgages at any time *between players' turns*. That is, as the dice are being passed from one player to another, you can say 'Hold it!', carry out your transaction, and then let the game proceed.
3   Private transactions can be discussed at any time, but can be carried out *only during the turn of either of the players involved*. Some players also allow such deals to be carried out between the turns of other players. To avoid any possibility of misunderstanding (not to say homicide) you should agree before the start of the game which rule you want to use.

The Monopoly Corollary

Any set of rules that can be printed on the small leaflet sold with the game needs occasional amplification

DOUBLES

If a player throws doubles he moves his token, as usual, the number of spaces indicated by the total of the two dice, and takes whatever action is appropriate to the space he lands on. However, his turn is not yet finished. He retains the dice and throws again. As before, he moves his token the indicated number of spaces and performs whatever actions may be required or permitted according to the space that is landed on.

If the second throw is also doubles, the player retains the dice and throws them a third time. If the third throw is *not* doubles, he moves his token, as before, takes the appropriate actions, and his turn ends.

If, however, he throws doubles three times in succession he does not move his token the number of spaces indicated by the third throw. Instead he lands in Jail. He must move his token directly to the space marked IN JAIL and his turn ends. He goes to Jail directly – that is, not proceeding round the board, not passing GO and not collecting £200 salary.

It must also be remembered that if a player ends up in Jail, by drawing a Chance or Community Chest card that sends him there, or by landing on the space marked GO TO JAIL, his turn ends immediately. This applies even if he has just thrown doubles.

One of the ways for a player to get out of Jail is by throwing doubles. For more information on this see the section on Jail on page 64.

LANDING ON UNOWNED PROPERTY
Buying

Whenever you land on a property that has not already been bought you may buy that property from the Bank at its printed price. The Banker gives you the Title Deed card showing ownership and you place it face-up in front of you.

You may buy a property in this way whether you land on the property by moving your token in accordance with the throw of the dice or whether you arrive there by following the instructions on a Chance or Community Chest card directing you to move your token to a particular space – for example, 'Advance to Mayfair'.

LANDING ON UNOWNED PROPERTY
Raising the Cash

Of course, if you decide to buy the property you have landed on you must first of all pay the Bank the full purchase price. If you do not have enough cash in hand, you may raise the cash you need in any of the following ways:

1. By selling back to the Bank any buildings you own on other Building Sites for one-half their list price.
2. By mortgaging any other property you own, so long as this property has no buildings on it.
3. By selling any other property you own to another player at whatever price you may agree between you.

Whatever means you use to acquire the cash needed to purchase the property in question you must pay the purchase price to the Bank before you receive the Title Deed.

So, for example, if you are buying Mayfair for £400 and you have only £200 in cash you must raise the additional £200 by one of the means described above. What you *cannot* do is get the Title Deed for Mayfair, mortgage it for £200, and use this £200 together with the £200 you had already to pay the purchase price.

Billing's Law

Live within your income, even if you have to borrow to do so

BUYING PROPERTY AT AUCTION

If a player lands on an unowned property and he decides not to buy it, the property must immediately be put up for auction. The Banker acts as auctioneer, and all players may bid for the property – including the player who has just landed on the property and has declined the opportunity of buying it at the printed price.

The bidding may start at any amount. So, in theory (if not very often in practice) you could buy a property at auction for as little as £1. The property goes to the player making the highest bid. The bid price must be handed over to the Bank before the player receives the Title Deed, and if the successful bidder does not have enough cash he may raise the additional cash needed by any of the means discussed in the previous section.

Corneille's Dictum

To win without risk is to triumph without glory

In the course of a game you may find examples of a property being sold at auction for much less than its printed price and examples of a property being sold at auction for many times its printed price. This is all part of the strategy of the game, discussed at length in the chapter *How To Win* (page 142).

BUYING PROPERTY AT AUCTION
Bankruptcy Auction

As well as the situation where a player decides not to buy an unowned property that he has landed on, there is one other situation where the Bank must put up property for auction. When a player owes the Bank more than he can pay (because of taxes or penalties) even when he has sold all his houses and hotels and mortgaged all his property, then he is bankrupt. He retires from the game and all his assets are taken over by the Bank. All the bankrupt player's mortgages are cancelled and the Title Deeds of the properties he owned are immediately put up for auction.

The official rules do not have much to say on this point, but the procedure here is important. The order in which the Banker puts the properties of a bankrupt player up for auction can affect the bidding strategy and may give an advantage to one player or another (including the Banker himself in his other role as a player). So to be perfectly fair there should be a predetermined rule to cover this situation. The fairest rule to follow is that these properties should be auctioned in descending order of value – the most expensive property being auctioned first and the least expensive last.

The Loser's Paradox

The only way to avoid mistakes . . .
is to gain experience
The only way to gain experience . . .
is to make mistakes

RENT

The rules say, 'When a player lands on owned property . . . the owner collects rent from him in accordance with the list printed on the Title Deed card applying to it. . . . If the site is mortgaged, no rent can be collected.'

The first thing to note is that you are liable for rent whenever you land on unmortgaged property owned by another player. It does not matter how you came to land there – whether you arrived at that space after moving your token in accordance with the throw of the dice or whether you were directed there by a Chance or Community Chest card, for example 'Go back to Old Kent Road'. The player who owns that property may demand rent from you in either case.

COMMUNITY CHEST

GO BACK TO OLD KENT ROAD

The next thing to note – and it is a very important point – is that in this situation although you are *liable* for rent, it is possible (and legal) to avoid paying it. If the owner notices that you have landed on his property and demands his due

RENT

rent then you *must* pay (or go bankrupt). But if he does not ask for the rent then you are under no compulsion to pay him. You do not have to call attention to the fact that you are occupying his property, and you do not have to volunteer to pay rent that has not been demanded. According to the rules, 'If the owner fails to ask for his rent before the next throw of the dice no rent may be collected.'

Durant's Discovery

One of the lessons of history is that nothing is often a good thing to do and always a clever thing to say

The moral is clear. If you land on another player's property say nothing – you may get away rent-free if your opponent is careless. Conversely, keep a close watch on the movements of your opponents' tokens, and never neglect to demand the rent that is due when they land on your property.

RENT
Inability to Pay

If you land on another player's property and you cannot afford the rent that is due, even after selling, mortgaging or trading all that you own, you will be bankrupt – unless you can make some sort of deal with your creditor whereby he will be satisfied with part payment of the debt. This situation is discussed in greater detail in the section on Bankruptcy (pages 92–5).

Beerbohm's Solace for the Vanquished

There is much to be said for failure. It is more interesting than success

Landing on mortgaged property

No rents may be collected for property that is mortgaged.

RENT
Rent for Building Sites

The rent that you have to pay when you land on a Building Site owned by another player depends on whether he owns all the lots of that colour group and, if so, whether he has erected any buildings on the site you have landed on.

Suppose you have landed on Marlborough Street, which is owned by one of your opponents.

MARLBOROUGH ST.

RENT	— site only	£14
,,	with 1 house	70
,,	,, 2 houses	200
,,	,, 3 houses	550
,,	,, 4 houses	750
,,	,, HOTEL	950

If a player owns *all* the sites of any Colour-Group, the rent is *doubled* on *unimproved* sites in that group

COST of houses — £100 each
,, ,, hotels — £100 plus 4 houses

MORTGAGE value of site £90

RENT
Rent for Building Sites

(a)   If your opponent *does not* own all three properties of the orange colour group – Bow Street and Vine Street as well as Marlborough Street – you pay only the basic rent printed on the Title Deed: £14.

(b)   If your opponent *does* own all three of the orange properties, and if he has not erected any houses on Marlborough Street, then the basic rent will be doubled. You will have to pay £28 for the privilege of landing there. This would hold true if there was a house on either Bow Street or Vine Street or on both of them.

    If your opponent has mortgaged either Bow Street or Vine Street, however, then he is not entitled to double rent on Marlborough Street – he is only entitled to the basic £14.

(c)   If your opponent has erected houses or a hotel on Marlborough Street he is entitled to charge you the rent applicable to the number of buildings he has erected, in accordance with the schedule printed on the Title Deed.

Bucy's Law

Nothing is ever accomplished by a reasonable man

The Monopoly Corollary

The totally rational player who never runs a risk, never wins

RENT
Rent for Utilities

If you land on either of the two Utilities on the board – the Electric Company or the Water Works – and it is owned by another player (and is not mortgaged) he may charge you rent. The rent that is payable depends on the numbers shown on the dice, and on whether your opponent owns only one or both of the Utilities.

(a) Suppose you throw a 2 and a 3. You move your five spaces and land on the Electric Company. This Utility is owned by one of your opponents, but he does not own the Water Works. The rent he may charge you is 4 times £5. That is, £20 rent.

(b) Suppose, as before, you have thrown a 2 and a 3 and landed on the Electric Company. Your opponent owns not only this Utility but the Water Works as well – and neither is mortgaged. The rent he may charge you this time is 10 times £5. The rent, because he owns both Utilities, is £50.

RENT
Rent for Railway Stations

There are four Railway Stations, one positioned on each side of the board. The basic rent payable for any one Railway Station is £25, but this increases with each additional Railway Station that is owned by the same player.

Suppose you land on Kings Cross Station. If this is owned by another player and is not mortgaged then he is entitled to charge you rent.

If this is the only Railway Station he owns you must pay him £25 rent. If he owns one other Railway Station, the rent you must pay him is £50. If he owns two other Railway Stations, the rent is £100. If he owns three other Railway Stations, the rent is £200.

Note, however, that these rents are applicable only if the other Railway Stations owned by this player are not mortgaged – mortgaged Railway Stations are not to be taken into account when assessing the rent payable.

Brandreth's Theory of Natural Justice

In Monopoly a belief in natural justice is entirely dependent on whether you own all four Railway Stations when your opponent lands on Kings Cross or he owns all four Railway Stations when you do

RENT
Rent for Railway Stations

FENCHURCH ST. STATION

BRITISH RAILWAYS

	£25
RENT	50
If 2 stations are owned	100
If 3 '' '' ''	200
If 4 '' '' ''	

MORTGAGE value — £100

MARYLEBONE STATION

BRITISH RAILWAYS

RENT	£25
If 2 stations are owned	50
If 3 '' '' ''	100
If 4 '' '' ''	200

MORT...

LIVERPOOL ST. STATION

BRITISH RAILWAYS

	£25
RENT	50
If 2 stations are owned	100
If 3 '' '' ''	200
If 4 '' '' ''	

MORTGAGE value — £100

KING'S CROSS STATION

BRITISH RAILWAYS

RENT	£25
If 2 stations are owned	50
If 3 '' '' ''	100
If 4 '' '' ''	200

MORTGAGE value — £100

TAXES

'In this world,' said Benjamin Franklin, 'nothing can be certain, except death and taxes'. Happily, in the world of Monopoly death is not inevitable, though taxes are.

There are two spaces on the board which involve payment of taxes – the INCOME TAX space and the SUPER TAX space.

If you land on the INCOME TAX space you must hand over £200 to the Bank – there goes your £200 for passing GO! Similarly, if you land on the SUPER TAX space you must give the Bank £100.

There is no right of appeal – you must pay up or go bankrupt.

The Song of the Taxed

I'm glad that I'm British,
I'm proud that I am free,
But I wish I were a little dog
And my tax man was a tree.

| INCOME TAX ◈ PAY £200 | SUPER TAX ◈ PAY £100 |

JAIL

The corner of the board occupied by the Jail is really two spaces in one – IN JAIL and JUST VISITING.

JAIL
Just Visiting

If you land on this space in the normal course of moving your token in accordance with the throw of the dice then you are Just Visiting. You place your token on the edge of the square, outside the Jail itself. You receive no penalties as a result of landing on this space, and you move off, as normal, on your next turn.

JAIL
Going To Jail

It is quite easy to land up IN JAIL. In the course of a game it is most unusual for a player to avoid being sent to Jail at some stage. Normally you will find yourself behind bars several times in the course of a game. There are three ways to get to Jail:

(a) By landing on the corner space that is marked GO TO JAIL.

(b) By drawing the Chance or Community Chest card that is marked 'Go To Jail'.

(c) By throwing doubles three times in succession.

    The rules say, 'When a player is sent to Jail his turn ends there. He cannot collect £200 salary in that move since, regardless of where his token is or of the path of the board, he must move his token directly into Jail.'

    So if you have landed on the GO TO JAIL space or drawn a Chance or Community Chest card directing you to 'Go To

COMMUNITY CHEST

GO TO JAIL
MOVE DIRECTLY TO JAIL
DO NOT PASS "GO"
DO NOT COLLECT £200

JAIL
Going To Jail

Jail' your turn ends even if you have just thrown doubles. You go *directly* to Jail without passing GO and without collecting £200 salary. Likewise, if you have thrown doubles for the third time in succession you do *not* advance your token the number of spaces shown by the dice on that throw but go directly to Jail.

The rules, however, may be a little misleading in one particular situation. Suppose your token is on Park Lane and you throw a 2 and a 3 to take you to the Community Chest space or you throw a 4 and a 6 to take you to the Chance space. You draw a card, and it says 'Go To Jail'. Fair enough, but you have just passed GO on that move. Do you collect your £200 salary?

Yes, you do, because you had passed GO *before* being sent to Jail. To avoid arguments, however, it is a good idea when in this situation to collect your £200 salary *before* you draw the Chance or Community Chest card.

Brandreth's Jailbird Paradox

At the start of the game, when you want most to keep moving round the board to acquire property, you will be sent to Jail constantly. Towards the end of the game, when you are on the brink of bankruptcy and desperate to be locked up for a while, there is no way you will land in Jail

JAIL
Getting Out Of Jail

Having landed in Jail how do you get out again? There are four ways of securing your release:

1. By throwing doubles on any of your next three turns after landing in Jail. If you get out of Jail by this method then you advance your token the number of spaces shown by the doubles throw. As in the normal situation when you throw doubles, you then have a further throw of the dice.

2. By using the 'Get Out Of Jail Free' card from the Chance or Community Chest pack if you have it. You show the card, replace it face down on the bottom of the appropriate pack, throw the dice and advance your token the number of spaces shown by the dice.

3. By purchasing a 'Get Out Of Jail Free' card from another player and using it as described above.

4. By paying a £50 fine. You may use this option on your first or second turn after landing in Jail. You pay your £50 to the Bank, throw the dice and advance your token accordingly.

COMMUNITY CHEST

GET OUT OF JAIL FREE

This card may be kept
until needed or sold

JAIL
Getting Out Of Jail

If you have not used any of the other methods of getting out of Jail then on your third throw after landing in Jail, if you have not thrown doubles you must immediately pay the £50 fine and move your token according to the total of the dice you have just thrown.

There is one point to be stressed here because it so often confuses players.

You must choose your option before throwing the dice, and there is no changing your mind afterwards. So if you decide to use a 'Get Out Of Jail Free' card or pay the £50 fine and then throw doubles, you are not entitled to claim your card or £50 back. Neither can you throw the dice to see if you get doubles on your first or second turn and then if you fail offer to pay the £50 fine to get out on that turn.

Ginsberg's Theorem of Despair

1   You can't win
2   You can't break even
3   You can't even quit the game

CHANCE AND COMMUNITY CHEST

There are three Chance spaces and three Community Chest spaces on the Monopoly board. When you land on one of these spaces you must take the top card from the appropriate pack. Turn it over, and you will find a set of instructions. With one exception – the 'Get Out Of Jail Free' card – these instructions should be followed at once. You must then return the card face down to the bottom of the pack.

The Darrow Conundrum

The Community Chest pack contains more bonus cards than penalty cards. The Chance pack, on the other hand, contains more penalty cards than bonus cards. Whether or not you feel this imbalance in the packs reflects reality will prove whether you are more inclined to believe in the possibility of a generous State than a benign Deity – or vice versa. If you are able to understand the conundrum and answer it, you are not only very clever, you are also in a position to discover whether instinctively you are an old-fashioned Marxist or an optimistic Believer

CHANCE AND COMMUNITY CHEST
Get Out Of Jail Free

There is one 'Get Out Of Jail Free' card in the Chance pack
and one in the Community Chest pack. If you draw one of
these cards keep it until you land in Jail, and then you have
the option of using the card to get out of Jail without paying
the usual £50 fine or having to wait until you throw doubles.
Alternatively you may sell the card to another player –
though you are unlikely to obtain as much as £50 for it. Only
when the card has been used to secure a free release from Jail
(or when the holder becomes bankrupt) is it returned to the
bottom of the pack it was taken from.

CHANCE

GET OUT OF JAIL FREE

This card may be kept
until needed or sold

CHANCE AND COMMUNITY CHEST
Bonuses and Fines

Over half the cards in the Chance and Community Chest packs relate to bonuses paid to you by the Bank (for example, 'Bank Pays You Dividend of £50') or penalties that you must pay to the Bank (for example, 'Pay Hospital £100').

COMMUNITY CHEST

BANK ERROR IN YOUR FAVOUR
COLLECT £200

CHANCE

PAY SCHOOL FEES
OF £150

CHANCE

YOUR BUILDING LOAN MATURES
RECEIVE £150

CHANCE AND COMMUNITY CHEST
Street or Property Repairs

The important point to remember when you draw either of these two penalty cards is that the amount you have to pay depends solely on the number of houses and hotels that you own *at the time you draw the card*.

CHANCE

YOU ARE ASSESSED FOR
STREET REPAIRS
£40 PER HOUSE
£115 PER HOTEL

CHANCE

MAKE GENERAL REPAIRS ON
ALL OF YOUR HOUSES
FOR EACH HOUSE PAY   £25
FOR EACH HOTEL PAY   £100

So if you draw the card which says 'You Are Assessed for Street Repairs . . .', and you do not own any houses or hotels, you get off scot free. Simply replace the card at the bottom of the pack. Suppose, however, that at the time you draw the card you own the following real estate:

Strand	with 4 houses
Fleet Street	with 4 houses
Trafalgar Square	with 1 hotel

You will have to work out your bill for street repairs as follows:

Strand	$4 \times £40 = £160$
Fleet Street	$4 \times £40 = £160$
Trafalgar Square	$1 \times £115 = £115$

Making a grand total (not so grand from your point of view) of £435.

Now suppose that you do not have quite enough ready cash to pay the bill, and that in order to raise the cash you have no option but to sell off some of your buildings, leaving you with:

Strand	with 3 houses
Fleet Street	with 3 houses
Trafalgar Square	with 4 houses

The question is: Now that the number of houses and hotels you own is different, are you still liable for the original street repairs bill of £435? The answer, alas, is that you are. The charges apply to the houses and hotels that you own at the time you draw the card.

CHANCE AND COMMUNITY CHEST
Go To Jail

There is one card in each of the packs which directs you to 'Go To Jail'. As directed by the card, you must go directly to Jail without passing GO and without collecting £200 salary. If, however, you have just passed GO on that move before landing on Chance or Community Chest you have already earned your £200 salary *before* being sent to Jail so you are entitled to collect it.

CHANCE

GO TO JAIL
MOVE DIRECTLY TO JAIL
DO NOT PASS "GO"
DO NOT COLLECT £200

CHANCE AND COMMUNITY CHEST
Other Chance and Community Chest Cards

The remaining Chance and Community Chest cards are those which instruct you to move your token around the board in some way. There is one Chance card that tells you to move your token backwards – 'Go back three spaces' – and one Community Chest card that says 'Go back to Old Kent Road'. With these two exceptions, you always move your token forward round the board (in the direction indicated by the arrow on the GO space).

There are two cards which direct you to 'Advance to GO'. If you draw either of these cards advance your token to the GO space and collect your £200 salary.

With all the other cards you move your token forward to the property specified on the card. For example, 'Advance to Trafalgar Square' or 'Take a trip to Marylebone Station'. In all cases, if as a result of following the instructions on the card you pass GO then you collect £200.

CHANCE

ADVANCE TO PALL MALL

IF YOU PASS "GO" COLLECT

£200

CHANCE AND COMMUNITY CHEST
Other Chance and Community Chest Cards

If the property you land on is unowned you may buy it, or if you decide not to buy it then the Bank must put it up for auction.

If the property you are directed to go to is owned by another player then you are liable to pay him rent, in just the same way as you would be if you had landed on that property as a result of moving your token in accordance with the throw of the dice.

George Eliot's Observation

Nothing is so good as it seems beforehand

The Monopoly Corollary

The Chance and Community Chest cards can be an anti-climax

FREE PARKING

The official rules have this to say about the FREE PARKING space, 'When, in the ordinary course of play, a player's token reaches this space, the player receives no benefit nor incurs any penalty, and moves ahead in the usual manner on his next turn.'

Many players, however, prefer to vary the rules so that all money paid by players in fines, taxes and building repairs is not paid to the Bank but is placed under the FREE PARKING space. A player landing on the FREE PARKING space collects whatever money has been placed there.

This, of course, is not the game according to the official rules. If you prefer to play this way nobody is going to stop you. All the same you must realize that playing the game this way changes its nature quite drastically. More money is in circulation so buildings get erected sooner, there is more emphasis placed on luck than on skill and, because of the location of the FREE PARKING space, being sent to Jail must be looked on more as an opportunity to win the FREE PARKING jackpot than as a punishment.

GO

The rules say, 'Every time that a player's token either lands on or passes over GO, while going in the direction of the Arrow, the Banker pays him £200 salary.'

Rent can be forfeited if you forget to ask for it. If a player's token lands on a property that is owned by you and you neglect to ask for the rent before the dice are thrown on the next turn, then you are no longer entitled to the rent that would have been due to you.

This is not the situation, however, in the case of the £200 salary for passing GO. You do not forfeit it if you forget to ask for it. It is the Banker's duty to pay you the £200 whenever you are entitled to it, without needing to be asked.

The Law of Duality

Of two possible events, only the undesired one will occur

The Monopoly Proof

When you are at Liverpool Street Station and your opponent has just built a hotel on Mayfair, you could throw a 5 and land on GO, but you'll throw a 4 without a doubt. Try it and see

BUYING AND ERECTING BUILDINGS
Houses

When you own all the properties in a colour group – for example, Old Kent Road and Whitechapel in the brown colour group or Regent Street, Oxford Street and Bond Street in the green colour group – you are allowed to start buying houses and erecting them on properties in this colour group.

As you can see from the schedule of rents on the Title Deed cards the rents increase sharply as you erect more houses on your properties. This is when the game really takes off.

Houses may be bought only from the Bank – you cannot acquire houses by trading with other players, and you cannot transfer houses from one site to another. The price you must pay for houses is marked on the Title Deeds. The prices of houses increase (as do property values) the further round the board you go.

For brown and light blue property groups – houses cost £50 each.

For crimson and orange property groups – houses cost £100 each.

For red and yellow property groups – houses cost £150 each.

For green and dark blue property groups – houses cost £200 each.

When there is a building shortage the Bank may have to auction houses if the demand exceeds the supply – see the section entitled *Building Shortage* (page 80). In this situation you can expect to pay somewhat more than the listed prices for the houses that you require.

The rules say, 'A player may buy and erect . . . at any time, except during an opponent's turn, as many houses as

BUYING AND ERECTING BUILDINGS
Houses

his judgment and financial standing will allow.' This should be interpreted to mean that you may buy houses at any time during your own turn or between the turns of other players – see page 44.

When you start erecting buildings on properties in a colour group none of those properties must be mortgaged. And you may not mortgage any property while any property in the same colour group has any buildings on it.

Suppose you own all the properties in the yellow colour group – Leicester Square, Coventry Street and Piccadilly – and you have mortgaged Leicester Square. If you wish to buy a house and erect it on Piccadilly, you must first lift the mortgage on Leicester Square. If later in the game you wish to mortgage any of the yellow properties, before you can do so you must sell the house on Piccadilly back to the Bank.

Another rule is that building must be done evenly. So:
1   You must have erected one house on every site of a colour group before you can erect a second house on any of them.
2   You must have two houses on every site before you can erect a third house on any one of them.
3   You must have three houses on every site before you can erect a fourth house on any one of them.
4   You must have four houses on every site before you can erect a hotel on any one of them.

Suppose you own the two properties of the brown colour group – Old Kent Road and Whitechapel Road. If you decide you can afford to erect two houses on this colour group then you must erect one house on each site. You may not have two houses on one site and none on the other as this breaks

BUYING AND ERECTING BUILDINGS
Houses

the rule about building evenly.

However this rule only applies to the buildings of an individual colour group. It is, for instance, quite permissible (if you own two complete colour groups) to have four houses on each property of one colour group and to have one house on each property of another colour group.

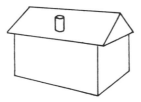

BUYING AND ERECTING BUILDINGS
Hotels

Because of the rule about building evenly, you can buy your first hotel for a colour group only when you have erected four houses on every property in that colour group. When you buy a hotel you pay the purchase price to the Bank, as listed on the property's Title Deed card, hand back to the Bank the four houses you have previously erected on that property and receive a hotel in exchange.

Only one hotel may be erected on any site.

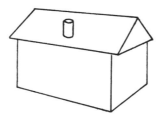

BUILDING SHORTAGE

The Monopoly set comes equipped with a limited number of buildings – 32 houses and 12 hotels. Although the Bank is assumed to have a limitless amount of cash, this is not the case with buildings. The fact that the Bank has only so many buildings for sale is an important element in the game, and has to be taken into account when planning your strategy.

The rules say, 'When the Bank has no Houses to sell, players wishing to build must wait for some player to turn back or to sell his Houses to the Bank before they can build. If there are a limited number of Houses and Hotels available, and two or more players wish to buy more than the Bank has, the Houses or Hotels must be sold at auction to the highest bidder.'

If you wish to buy and erect a house at a time when the Bank has no houses to sell you will just have to be patient and wait until houses are returned to the Bank by some other player.

Remember, houses may only be bought from the Bank. You are not allowed to transfer buildings from one site to another or to buy them from another player.

The situation may occur where the Bank has no houses for

A Home Truth

Patience is a virtue

The Monopoly Corollary

Being virtuous is often frustrating and not always fun

BUILDING SHORTAGE

sale but does have several hotels. Suppose you own the complete group of light blue properties, for instance, and you have erected three houses on each. You have plenty of cash available so you would like to erect hotels on all three of these properties. If there were no building shortage there would be no problem. If you had *four* houses on each property there would be no problem. But because you have only three houses on each site and the Bank has no houses for sale you cannot erect hotels – although the Bank has hotels for sale!

This apparently paradoxical situation arises because the rules say unarguably that before you can buy and erect hotels you must have four houses on each site. You will just have to wait until other players return three or more houses to the Bank.

BUILDING SHORTAGE
Buildings Sold at Auction

If the Bank has a limited number of houses (or hotels) available to sell, and more than one player wants to buy them, the Bank must put the buildings up for auction and sell them to the highest bidder.

When buildings are sold by auction there is no minimum price and no ceiling. So in theory you can buy buildings at auction more cheaply than you would otherwise. But in practice you will find that you will always pay more at auction than you would otherwise. This illustrates one of the classic laws of economics – where demand exceeds supply, prices are pushed up.

Suppose the Bank has only one house for sale. You want to buy it for Euston Road (where houses normally cost £50) and your opponent wants to buy it for Park Lane (where houses normally cost £200). Your opponent is obviously going to be prepared to pay £200 and possibly more. So if you are really determined to have that house you are going to have to pay many times the normal price of £50. If, on the

---

Glasgow's Law

There's something wrong if you're always right

The Monopoly Corollary

If you always win at Monopoly there can only be three explanations:
  1   You cheat
  2   Your opponents feel sorry for you
  3   You haven't played very many games so far

BUILDING SHORTAGE
Buildings Sold at Auction

other hand, you decide that you will stop bidding at £50 you are giving your opponent the opportunity to buy it for £51 – much less than the £200 he would have had to pay normally for a house on Park Lane.

When buildings are being sold by auction the bidder who wants to erect the house on the more expensive property is always at an advantage.

Houses must always be auctioned one at a time and it is not necessary for a player to mention which property he has in mind for a house before the bidding starts.

MORTGAGES

One way of raising extra cash is by borrowing money from the Bank by mortgaging some of your property. (You are not allowed to borrow money from the Bank except by means of a mortgage. Nor are you allowed to borrow money from other players under any conditions.)

You may mortgage property at any stage of the game either during your own turn or between the turns of other players.

Any property (including Utilities and Railway Stations) may be mortgaged. But you are not allowed to mortgage a property while you have any buildings standing on it or while you have any buildings standing on any other property in the same colour group. If you own a complete colour group with buildings on any of the sites then you must sell all the buildings on that colour group back to the Bank before you can mortgage any of the properties in that colour group.

Once a property has been mortgaged you may not erect any buildings on any property of that colour group until the mortgage has been lifted.

The mortgage value of each site is printed on the Title Deed card. To mortgage a property you show the Banker the Title Deed and ask him to give you the mortgage value. You then replace the Title Deed card *face down* in front of you.

MORGAGES
The Effect of Mortgages on Rent

Rent is not payable on properties that are mortgaged. So if you own Fleet Street, for instance, but have mortgaged it, then your opponent does not have to pay you any rent when he lands on Fleet Street.

If a property is mortgaged it also affects the rent that is due on other properties in the same group. This also applies to the Utilities and Railway Stations.

If you own a complete colour group you are entitled to double the basic rent for unimproved properties in that group. But if you own a complete colour group and have mortgaged one of the properties you are *not* entitled to double the basic rent if your opponent lands on one of the unmortgaged properties in that group – you are only entitled to the basic rent.

If you own both Utilities and have mortgaged one of them, you are only entitled to a rent of 4 times – not 10 times – the value shown on the dice if your opponent lands on the Utility that is not mortgaged.

If you own two or more Railway Stations and you have mortgaged any of them this affects the amount of rent you collect if your opponent lands on one of your unmortgaged Railway Stations. The rent is calculated according to the number of *unmortgaged* Railway Stations you own.

MORTGAGES
Lifting a Mortgage

In order to lift a mortgage you must repay the Bank the amount you borrowed (the mortgage value as printed on the Title Deed) plus 10 per cent interest on the mortgage value.

For example, if you mortgaged Coventry Street you would receive £130 from the Bank. To lift the mortgage you must repay the Bank £130 plus £13 interest – that is, £143 in total.

Having repaid the Bank you turn the Title Deed card face up again. The restrictions that applied while the property was mortgaged – on collecting rent for the site and in erecting buildings if this was part of a complete colour group – now no longer apply.

MORGAGES
Transferring a Property

As part of a private transaction you may sell a mortgaged property to another player (for any price agreed between the two of you) or exchange it for some other property.

When a mortgaged property is transferred from one player to another, the player who receives it has two options:

(a) He may lift the mortgage immediately, paying the Bank the mortgage value of the property plus 10 per cent interest in the normal manner.

(b) If he does not wish to lift the mortgage immediately, he must nevertheless pay the Bank 10 per cent interest on the mortgage value of the property. This is the Bank's fee for permitting the transfer. If the player decides to lift the mortgage later he must still pay 10 per cent interest on top of the mortgage value.

If you have the cash available, lift the mortgage at the time the mortgaged property is transferred. Otherwise it costs more.

The First Law of Consolation

Since we learn from our mistakes, every defeat at Monopoly contributes immeasurably to our general education

SELLING BUILDINGS

If you find yourself short of cash you may have to sell houses or hotels back to the Bank. The rules say, 'Houses and Hotels may be resold by players to the Bank only, but this may be done at any time and the Bank will pay one half of the price paid for them.' Note that you are not allowed to sell or transfer buildings to another player, and you are not allowed to move buildings from one property to another.

There are two items in the rule about selling buildings that require clarification. The rules say that buildings may be sold back to the Bank *'at any time'*. This should be taken to mean at any time during your own turn or between the turns of other players. The rules also say that buildings are sold back to the Bank for 'one half of *the price paid for them'*. This should be taken to mean one half of *the normal price as printed on the Title Deed card*. This interpretation is necessary because buildings may be purchased for vastly different prices when they are sold by auction. If the rules were to be interpreted literally then a careful record would need to be kept of the price paid for each building at auction, so that when these buildings were sold back to the Bank the player would receive one half of the price paid at auction – and such a system would be almost unworkable and certainly open to abuse.

The price of a house erected on the dark blue property group, for instance, is £200. So whenever you sell back to the Bank a house from this colour group you will receive £100. If, later in the game, you decide to re-erect a house on this colour group you will once again have to pay the full price of £200.

The rules about erecting buildings evenly on the properties of a colour group also apply in reverse when you

SELLING BUILDINGS

are selling buildings back to the Bank.

Suppose you own the following properties:

Pall Mall   with 2 houses
Whitehall   with 2 houses
Northumberland Avenue   with 3 houses.

If you wish to sell one house from this property group, then you must sell one of the houses from Northumberland Avenue.

SELLING BUILDINGS
Selling Hotels

The cost of a hotel is equivalent to the cost of five houses.

If you need a lot of money, you may sell a hotel for a sum equal to one half of the cost of five houses. If you do this you will also have to sell buildings from the other properties in this colour group because of the rule about building evenly.

You may, instead, convert a hotel into four houses and receive from the Bank one half of the cost of a house for that colour group.

Or you may pursue a course between these two extremes. You may, for example, convert each hotel on a colour group to three houses or two houses or one house.

SELLING BUILDINGS
The Effect of a Building Shortage

If the Bank has a limited supply of houses to sell then your options may be severely curtailed when it comes to selling hotels.

Suppose the Bank has only five houses for sale. You own the orange property group – Bow Street, Marlborough Street and Vine Street – with a hotel on each. You are rather short of cash so you would like to convert each of these hotels to four houses. Sadly you can't do it – the Bank just doesn't have the houses available. The best you can do is to convert the three hotels to five houses.

You are selling to the Bank the equivalent of fifteen houses and receiving back five houses. So the cash you get is one-half the cost of 10 houses at £100 each. That is, £500 in total.

Of course the five houses you get from the Bank will have to be erected evenly – one house on one of the properties and two houses on each of the others.

Brandreth's Law of Failure

If in real life you're a born loser, you'll find that Monopoly is just like real life

BANKRUPTCY

A player is bankrupt when he owes more than he can pay either to another player or to the Bank. When you are bankrupt you are out of the game: you have lost.

BANKRUPTCY
Trying to Avoid Bankruptcy

When you do not have enough cash to pay what you owe to another player or to the Bank you will have to attempt to raise the money by selling buildings back to the Bank and by mortgaging property or selling it to other players. You are not allowed to borrow money from other players, or to borrow money from the Bank except by means of a mortgage.

If the Bank is your creditor then the amount you owe must be paid in full. If your creditor is another player, however, you may attempt to make a deal with him whereby he will accept some of your property in settlement of the debt, leaving you solvent and still in the game. It may sometimes be in his interests to do so.

Hazlitt's Law of Last-minute Defeat

One is always more vexed at losing a game of any sort by a single hole or ace, than if one has never had a chance of winning

BANKRUPTCY
Going Bankrupt

If you are not able to raise the money to clear the debt – after selling or mortgaging all your assets – then you are bankrupt.

The Bankrupt's Cry

Don't try to make a fool out of me . . .
I'm doing all right by myself

If your debt is to another player, you must hand over to that player everything that you have of value – all your cash, including cash raised from the sale of buildings back to the Bank, and all your Title Deeds. Your creditor may not claim the balance of the debt from the Bank or any other source.

If the assets you hand over include mortgaged property your creditor has two options:
(a) He may lift the mortgage on the property immediately, paying the Bank the mortgage value of the property plus 10 per cent interest.
(b) If he does not wish to lift the mortgage immediately, he must nevertheless pay the Bank 10 per cent interest on

An Alcoholics Anonymous Dictum

Misery is optional

The Monopoly Corollary

When you've just gone bankrupt, it isn't

BANKRUPTCY
Going Bankrupt

the mortgage value of the property. If he decides to lift the mortgage later he must pay a further 10 per cent on top of the mortgage value.

If your debt is to the Bank, instead of another player, you hand over all your assets to the Bank. If you have a 'Get Out Of Jail Free' card it is returned to the bottom of the appropriate pack. The Bank cancels any outstanding mortgages on the property you have handed over, and immediately auctions off to the other players the Title Deeds you have handed over.

TRADING

Private transactions between players are allowed – within limits. They are not allowed in championship games.

Any such transactions may be discussed at any time but should only be carried out either during the turn of one of the players involved or between the turns of other players.

Buildings may never be transferred from one player to another. Property, however, whether mortgaged or unmortgaged, may be transferred – subject to the rule that when mortgaged property is transferred the player who receives it has the option of either lifting the mortgage immediately by paying the Bank the mortgage value plus 10 per cent interest or just paying the transfer fee of 10 per cent of the mortgage value.

Property may be sold or traded between players in this way at whatever prices they may agree between them.

The extent to which other horse-trading is permissible is a controversial issue. Unless you have clear house rules, you should agree beforehand what is and is not allowed. For example, do you allow deals such as the following?

(a) Player A, who owns Park Lane and Mayfair, agrees with player B that for £500 now, he will exempt player B from any future rents when he lands on these properties.

The Quiet Trader's Tactic

When doing a deal and needing to be as deceptive as possible, speak as softly as you can and directly into your opponent's ear. People will believe almost anything if you whisper it

TRADING

(b)   When there is a building shortage, player A offers
      player B a choice property or a sum of money if player A
      will sell some of his houses back to the Bank so player B
      may buy them.

Whether or not you allow deals like these there is one kind
of deal that is always taboo – and that's a deal involving
considerations that have no connection with the game. For
example, a father should never say to his son, 'If you give me
Bond Street, son, I'll give you Kings Cross Station and let
you stay up till eleven o'clock.'

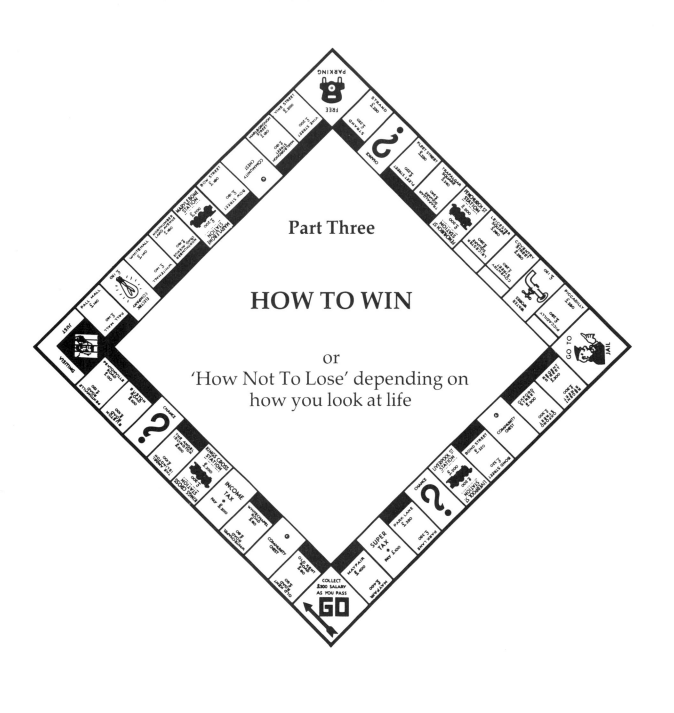

Part Three

HOW TO WIN

or
'How Not To Lose' depending on
how you look at life

THE EMOTIONAL FACTOR
Characteristics that make for a Monopoly Winner

1   A good memory
2   An ability to concentrate
3   Nerve
4   Stamina
5   Immense patience
6   Single-mindedness
7   A poker face
8   Ruthlessness
9   A good digestive system
10   Being either a Leo or a Scorpio

THE EMOTIONAL FACTOR
Characteristics that make for a Monopoly Loser

1   Lack of self-discipline
2   An overwhelming desire to be loved
3   Greed
4   A keen sense of humour
5   Impetuosity
6   Shortsightedness
7   A face that reveals everything
8   Excitability
9   A frequent need for comfort breaks
10 Being either a Cancerian or a Piscean

KEEP YOUR EYE ON THE ACTION

You can improve your chance of winning simply by paying close attention to what is happening in the game. With concentration, you can avoid careless mistakes – and take advantage of mistakes made by your opponents.

The prime example of a careless mistake is not noticing when your opponent lands on your property and letting him go rent-free. With a little care you will *never* let an opponent escape paying rent.

Yogi Berra's Law

You can observe a lot just by watching

When you land on a property owned by one of your opponents don't pay him any more rent than you need to. For example, you may land on Whitechapel Road on which your opponent has erected one house, and he may say, 'That's £60 rent you owe me!' Don't take his word for it – look at his Title Deed card and check that he is not claiming more rent than he is entitled to. In fact the rent for Whitechapel Road with one house is £20, not £60.

Whenever you are handed cash – either from an opponent or from the Banker – always count it yourself. If there is a mistake in your favour there is no need to say anything; anyone who makes such a careless mistake in a cut-throat game like Monopoly deserves to lose by it. But if there is a mistake in the other person's favour be sure to kick up a fuss and demand what is rightfully yours.

You should also try to be aware at all times of the status of each of your opponents:

KEEP YOUR EYE ON THE ACTION

1   How much cash does he have?
2   Which properties does he own?
3   Which of his properties are mortgaged?
4   Which properties does he need to acquire in order to get control of complete colour groups?
5   What rents will you have to pay if you land on any of his properties?
   You should also be constantly aware of the following factors in the game:
1   Which of your opponents is in the strongest position and who is the weakest?
2   How many buildings does the Bank have left? Is there any prospect of a building shortage?
   Knowing the answers to all these questions is essential for successful play. All this information has to be weighed in the balance when you are formulating your own strategy.

Clarence Darrow's Observation

History repeats itself. That's one of the things wrong with history

Charles Darrow's Refutation

When you play Monopoly history won't repeat itself – unless yours is a lousy memory

DICE AND PROBABILITY

Situations often occur in Monopoly where it is useful to be able to calculate the probability of your opponent landing on your property. For example, there is a better than even chance that on his next move he will land on a property group owned by you, this might be a good time to erect a few extra buildings on those properties.

Similarly you may calculate the probability that you will land on a high-rent group of properties owned by your opponent on *your* next throw. If there is a high probability that this will happen it might be wise to defer any expenditure so that you keep enough cash ready to pay the rent. On the other hand, if the probability is low that you will land on your opponent's high-rent properties, you may decide that there is no need to maintain a cash reserve to cover that unlikely eventuality.

A move is determined in Monopoly by throwing two dice. Each of the dice can show any number from 1 to 6, so with two dice there are thirty-six different combinations. Assuming that the dice are properly made and are not weighted, each of the thirty-six combinations is equally likely.

The Cardsharp Code

A Smith and Wesson beats four aces

The Monopoly Corollary

And a weighted dice wins you the game –
provided it's yours

DICE AND PROBABILITY

The total value of the two dice may be any number from 2 to 12, and you can see from the table of possible combinations that not all total values are equally likely. For instance, you can get a total value of 12 in only one way – by throwing 6-6. However, you can get a total value of 7 in six different ways – by throwing 1-6, 2-5, 3-4, 4-3, 5-2 or 6-1. Therefore over a large number of throws you will get a total of 7 with the dice six times more often than you will get a total of 12.

The probability of getting each total is as follows:

Total of throw	Probability	
2	1/36	
3	2/36	(1/18)
4	3/36	(1/12)
5	4/36	(1/9)
6	5/36	
7	6/36	(1/6)
8	5/36	
9	4/36	(1/9)
10	3/36	(1/12)
11	2/36	(1/18)
12	1/36	

From this you can see that 7 is the most commonly thrown total – you have a one-in-six chance of throwing it. Other totals are less probable the farther they are from 7.

DICE AND PROBABILITY

Don Quixote's Motto

They who lose today may win tomorrow

WHICH PROPERTIES ARE LANDED ON MOST OFTEN?

Just as certain totals are more likely to be thrown with the dice than others, you will also find that some parts of the board are landed on more often than others.

For instance, player's tokens often occupy the GO and IN JAIL spaces. Every player starts the game on GO, and there are two cards in the Chance and Community Chest decks that send a player to GO. Similarly the probability of landing on the IN JAIL space is quite high – you can get there by throwing three consecutive doubles, landing on GO TO JAIL, or drawing a 'Go To Jail' card from the Chance or Community Chest decks.

So, taking into account that players' tokens are fairly often on GO or IN JAIL and that 7, 6, 8, 5 and 9 are the totals most often thrown with the dice, you can see from the layout of the board that the light blue and the orange property groups

The First Law of Computers

To err is human.
To really foul things up needs a computer

The Monopoly Corollary

If you use a pocket calculator to calculate the chances of your opponent landing on Kings Cross Station, he will land on Mayfair (on which you have just built a hotel) at the very moment you are completing your calculation – and you won't notice

WHICH PROPERTIES ARE LANDED ON MOST OFTEN?

and Kings Cross and Marylebone stations must also have a higher than average chance of being landed on.

Of course this is just taking into account the first throw after landing on GO or IN JAIL. There are a lot of other considerations to be taken into account – combinations of throws, for instance, and other properties you can have your token sent to by a Chance or Community Chest card. Analyzing all these factors, it seems that the ten properties landed on most often are:

Trafalgar Square	Red group
Fenchurch Street Station	
Marlborough Street	Orange group
Vine Street	Orange group
Kings Cross Station	
Bow Street	Orange group
Water Works	
Marylebone Station	
Euston Road	Light blue group
The Angel, Islington	Light blue group

Naturally, the fact that these properties are the ones that are most often landed on makes them very desirable properties to own.

It is worth memorizing this list and using the information when deciding:
(a) Which properties you should buy.
(b) Which properties to trade.
(c) Which properties to develop if you have a choice of colour groups.
(d) Which properties to mortgage if you need to raise cash.

WHICH PROPERTIES ARE LANDED ON MOST OFTEN?

The Paturi Principle

Success is the result of behaviour that completely contradicts the usual expectations about the behaviour of a successful person

The Monopoly Corollary

You can ignore every one of these strategies, disregard all this sound advice – and still win the game. If you're lucky

WHICH ARE THE BEST PROPERTIES TO OWN?

Let us look at all the different properties and examine the factors that affect their desirability.

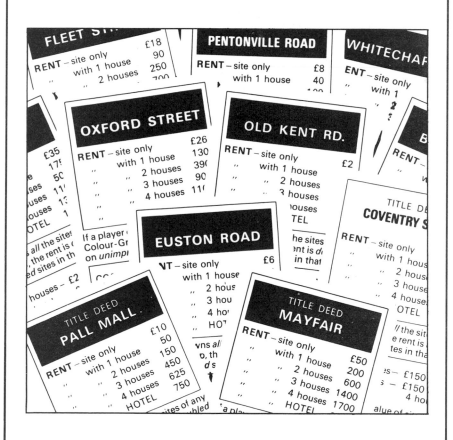

WHICH ARE THE BEST PROPERTIES TO OWN?
Utilities

They are fairly inexpensive – £150 each. The Water Works has an above-average chance of being landed on, and the Electric Company has an average chance of being landed on. The big disadvantage with the Utilities is that they cannot be developed to bring in bigger rents, so they are relatively worthless when developed colour groups start producing big rents.

WHICH ARE THE BEST PROPERTIES TO OWN?
Railway Stations

At £200 they are average-cost properties. Three of the Railway Stations – Kings Cross, Marylebone and Fenchurch Street – have an above-average chance of being landed on. The other – Liverpool Street – has a below-average chance of being landed on. The rent they bring in is significant if three or four are owned, but not so exciting if only one or two are owned. Like the Utilities, they suffer from the disadvantage that they cannot be developed. They lose their value later in the game, when the rent they produce begins to seem small in comparison with the rent produced by developed building sites.

WHICH ARE THE BEST PROPERTIES TO OWN?
Colour Groups

The only way to bring in really big rents is by owning and developing one or more complete colour groups of building sites. The relative desirability of the different colour groups depends on a number of factors:

The probability of the properties being landed on.

From this point of view, the best colour groups are the orange, light blue and red groups. The worst are the greens and dark blues.

The cost of the properties.

The less expensive the property the more cash you should have available to buy buildings to develop the property group quickly. But you have to set against this the fact that the more expensive the property is the higher the rent when that property is landed on.

The cost of houses.

If the houses are inexpensive you can develop your colour group more quickly. If the houses are costly it will take you much longer to develop your properties, but you will get higher rents.

It should be noted that the cost of houses is the same for any two colour groups on the same side of the board – for instance, houses cost £50 each for the brown and light blue groups, £100 each for the crimson and orange groups. But for the more expensive of the two groups the increase in rental value as a result of buying a house is greater. A £100 house, in that sense, is worth more on an orange property than a £100 house on a crimson property. Considered only from the point of view of house costs, the light blue group has an advantage over the brown group, the orange group has the advantage over the crimson group, the yellow over the red, and the dark blue over the green.

WHICH ARE THE BEST PROPERTIES TO OWN?
So Which are Best?

Pulling all this information together, we can grade all the properties in order of desirability. The table below shows the most desirable properties at the top and the least desirable at the bottom.

Property desirability

1. Light blue and orange groups
2. Crimson and red groups
3. Yellow and dark blue groups
4. Green and brown groups
5. Three or four Railway Stations
6. Two Utilities
7. Two Railway Stations
8. One Utility
9. One Railway Station
10. Single Building Sites (not in complete group)

THE UTILITIES STRATEGY

The Utilities are generally regarded as the poorest investments on the board. That reputation is not entirely deserved.

It is true that ownership of the Water Works and the Electric Company is not essential if you are to win the game. Your chances of winning are almost always going to depend on getting complete colour groups of building sites and on the number of buildings you can erect. So is it worthwhile buying the Utilities if you land on them?

The Utilities cost £150 each. The rent that is payable when a Utility is landed on is four times the amount shown on the dice if one Utility is owned, or ten times the amount shown on the dice if both Utilities are owned by the same player. The minimum amount the dice can show is 2, the maximum is 12, and the average (and most frequent) amount the dice can show is 7. The following table summarizes the essential facts:

	Cost	Minimum rent	Maximum rent	Average rent
1 Utility owned	£150	£8	£48	£28
2 Utilities owned	£300	£20	£120	£70

So if you own one Utility your opponents are, on average, going to have to land on it six times before you start making a profit on your investment. But bear in mind that the Water Works is one of the ten most-landed-on spaces on the board! If you own both Utilities the figures are much better – your

THE UTILITIES STRATEGY

opponents need, on average, only to land on *either one of them* five times before you start making a clear profit.

Compare these figures with the figures for a single Railway Station. This costs £200, and the rent is £25. So your opponents will have to land on it *nine* times before you are making a profit. Or compare them with the figures for a single building site that does not form part of a complete colour group. For instance, if you own only Vine Street in the orange property group, it will have cost you £200 and the rent is £16. So your opponents must land on it *thirteen* times before you show a profit.

These figures reveal that the Utilities are not such a bad investment after all. Certainly they don't compare with a complete property group or all the Railway Stations, but they are a better investment than a single Railway Station or a single building site.

Bearing these facts in mind, Brandreth's recommended strategy for the Utilities is as follows:

1   If you land on either of the Utilities *early in the game*, buy it. If you get the chance to buy both, do so.

    Alternatively, if you have nerves of steel, when you land on an unowned Utility early in the game, decline the opportunity to buy it. When the Bank sells it by auction, as it must, be prepared to bid up to £150 for it. Usually your opponents will not be prepared to bid very highly, and you will often acquire the Utility for less than the listed price of £150.

    However, if you already own one Utility and you land on the other, it is probably safer to buy it outright, rather than risk an opponent forcing up the bidding at auction to stop you having both Utilities.

THE UTILITIES STRATEGY

2 If one of your opponents lands on a Utility at an early stage of the game and does not wish to buy it, be prepared to bid up to £150 for it in the ensuing auction – especially if you already own the other Utility.

3 If the Utilities come up for sale late in the game, unless you have a mass of spare cash, don't buy them.

4 In the later stages of the game, when you have one or more complete groups of building sites, you should concentrate on developing these. The Utilities should now be regarded as disposable. If you can, trade them for properties which will give you complete colour groups. Or mortgage them, if you have any property with two houses on it, in order to erect the third house – but make sure you mortgage single Railway Stations and single building sites first.

Barzun's Law of Learning

The simple but difficult arts of paying attention, copying accurately, following an argument, detecting an ambiguity or a false inference, testing guesses by summoning up contrary instances, organizing one's time and one's thought for study – all these arts cannot be taught in the air but only through the difficulties of a defined subject; they cannot be taught in one course or one year, but must be acquired gradually in dozens of connections

THE RAILWAY STATIONS STRATEGY

The rent for Railway Stations increases according to the number you own:

£25 if you own 1 Railway Station
£50 if you own 2 Railway Stations
£100 if you own 3 Railway Stations
£200 if you own 4 Railway Stations

Whether or not the Railway Stations are a sound investment will depend on how many you own. Owning a single Railway Station is a poor investment, two is not quite so bad, but you have to own three or preferably all four to make your investment really pay.

Three of the Railway Stations have a statistically better-than-average chance of being landed on – Kings Cross, Marylebone and Fenchurch Street. Liverpool Street has a worse-than-average chance of being landed on. If you own the three better Railway Stations or all four, you are assured of a nice steady income of £100 or £200 each time any of them is landed on. This is especially advantageous in the early and middle stages of the game, but declines in importance once developed building sites start producing much higher rents.

The problem is that in the early stages of the game you can not always be sure whether buying a Railway Station is going to be a good investment because you don't know how many you are eventually going to wind up with. However, some general guidelines can be laid down. If you have the opportunity to buy a Railway Station, you should do so if:

(a)   No Railway Stations are owned by any of your opponents.

(b)   Only one Railway Station is owned by another player.

If one of your opponents already owns two or three

THE RAILWAY STATIONS STRATEGY

Railway Stations you may decide to buy this one to prevent him from getting his hands on it – or you can let it be sold at auction if you are sure another player will outbid him.

   If two or three of your opponents each own one Railway Station, you should never buy another unless you have plenty of spare cash. If your cash is limited there are better ways of spending it.

The Price Gambit

When attempting to buy the Railway Station you need from a player in financial difficulties remember: it's worth 200, he'll ask for 150, offer him 50, he'll take 100

The Napoleonic Warning

Unhappy the general who comes on the field of battle with a system

Brandreth's Defence of the Railway Stations Strategy

Who won the Battle of Waterloo?

PROPERTY DEVELOPMENT STRATEGY

The key to winning at Monopoly is owning complete colour groups of properties and erecting as many buildings as you can as quickly as possible in order to collect high rents.

Unfortunately, achieving this is not as simple as it sounds.

1   You do not have a free hand in deciding which properties to acquire. You may only acquire unowned properties you land on, properties which are sold by auction, or properties you can obtain from other players by trading.

2   You are constrained by the amount of cash you have. You have to make decisions as to whether or not you can afford to buy property and whether or not you can afford to buy buildings. You must nearly always keep a cash reserve adequate enough to cover any likely expenditure such as fines or rent when you land on another player's property.

3   You must always bear in mind that your opponents are probably as keen to win as you are. They are going to do all they can to foul up your plans. As well as pursuing your own objectives, you must be aware of what your opponents are planning – and try to stop them.

PROPERTY DEVELOPMENT STRATEGY
Property Development Tables

These tables show the costs of building houses and hotels for each property, the rent that results from each stage of development, and the percentage return on the investment. This latter figure is not a 'true' percentage return, as it is based only on the cost of a single property and the buildings erected on it – it does not take into account the necessary investment in the other sites of the same group. The figures given, however, are more useful as a means of comparing the profitability of investment in different building sites and the profitability of different stages in development of any single site.

The Ashley-Perry Statistical Axioms

1   Numbers are tools, not rules.
2   Numbers are symbols for things; the number and the thing are not the same.
3   Skill in manipulating numbers is a talent, not evidence of divine guidance.
4   Like other occult techniques of divination, the statistical method has a private jargon deliberately contrived to obscure its methods from non-practitioners.
5   The product of arithmetical computation is the answer to an equation; it is not the solution to a problem.

PROPERTY DEVELOPMENT STRATEGY
Brown Property Group

	Old Kent Road	Whitechapel Road
Purchase price	£60	£60
Basic rent	£2	£4
	Houses cost £50 each Hotels cost £250 each (£50 plus 4 houses)	

OLD KENT ROAD

	Cumulative development cost £	Rent £	Percentage return on investment
Site only	60	4	6.67
1 house	110	10	9.09
2 houses	160	30	18.75
3 houses	210	90	42.85
4 houses	260	160	61.54
Hotel	310	250	80.64

WHITECHAPEL ROAD

	Cumulative development cost £	Rent £	Percentage return on investment
Site only	60	8	13.33
1 house	110	20	18.18
2 houses	160	60	37.50
3 houses	210	180	85.71
4 houses	260	320	123.08
Hotel	310	450	145.16

PROPERTY DEVELOPMENT STRATEGY
Light Blue Property Group

	The Angel	Euston Road	Pentonville Road
Purchase price	£100	£100	£120
Basic rent	£6	£6	£8

Houses cost £50 each Hotels cost £250 each (£50 plus 4 houses)

THE ANGEL and EUSTON ROAD

	Cumulative development cost £	Rent £	Percentage return on investment
Site only	100	12	12.0
1 house	150	30	20.0
2 houses	200	90	45.0
3 houses	250	270	108.0
4 houses	300	400	133.33
Hotel	350	550	157.14

PENTONVILLE ROAD

	Cumulative development cost £	Rent £	Percentage return on investment
Site only	120	16	13.33
1 house	170	40	23.53
2 houses	220	100	45.46
3 houses	270	300	111.11
4 houses	320	450	140.63
Hotel	370	600	162.16

PROPERTY DEVELOPMENT STRATEGY
Crimson Property Group

	Pall Mall	Whitehall	Northumberland Avenue
Purchase price	£140	£140	£160
Basic rent	£10	£10	£12
	Houses cost £100 each Hotels cost £500 each (£100 plus 4 houses)		

PALL MALL and WHITEHALL

	Cumulative development cost £	Rent £	Percentage return on investment
Site only	140	20	14.29
1 house	240	50	20.83
2 houses	340	150	44.12
3 houses	440	450	102.27
4 houses	540	625	115.74
Hotel	640	750	117.19

NORTHUMBERLAND AVENUE

	Cumulative development cost £	Rent £	Percentage return on investment
Site only	160	24	15.0
1 house	260	60	23.08
2 houses	360	180	50.0
3 houses	460	500	108.70
4 houses	560	700	125.0
Hotel	660	900	136.36

PROPERTY DEVELOPMENT STRATEGY
Orange Property Group

	Bow Street	Marlborough Street	Vine Street
Purchase price	£180	£180	£200
Basic rent	£14	£14	£16

Houses cost £100 each Hotels cost £500 each (£100 plus 4 houses)

BOW STREET and MARLBOROUGH STREET

	Cumulative development cost £	Rent £	Percentage return on investment
Site only	180	28	15.56
1 house	280	70	25.0
2 houses	380	200	52.63
3 houses	480	550	114.58
4 houses	580	750	129.31
Hotel	680	950	139.70

VINE STREET

	Cumulative development cost £	Rent £	Percentage return on investment
Site only	200	32	16.0
1 house	300	80	26.67
2 houses	400	220	55.0
3 houses	500	600	120.0
4 houses	600	800	133.33
Hotel	700	1000	142.86

PROPERTY DEVELOPMENT STRATEGY
Red Property Group

	Strand	Fleet Street	Trafalgar Square
Purchase price	£220	£220	£240
Basic rent	£18	£18	£20
	Houses cost £150 each Hotels cost £750 each (£150 plus 4 houses)		

STRAND and FLEET STREET

	Cumulative development cost £	Rent £	Percentage return on investment
Site only	220	36	16.36
1 house	370	90	24.32
2 houses	520	250	48.08
3 houses	670	700	104.48
4 houses	820	875	106.70
Hotel	970	1050	108.25

TRAFALGAR SQUARE

	Cumulative development cost £	Rent £	Percentage return on investment
Site only	240	40	16.67
1 house	390	100	25.64
2 houses	540	300	55.56
3 houses	690	750	108.70
4 houses	840	925	110.12
Hotel	990	1100	111.11

PROPERTY DEVELOPMENT STRATEGY
Yellow Property Group

	Leicester Square	Coventry Street	Piccadilly
Purchase price	£260	£260	£280
Basic rent	£22	£22	£24
	Houses cost £150 each Hotels cost £750 each (£150 plus 4 houses)		

LEICESTER SQUARE and COVENTRY STREET

	Cumulative development cost £	Rent £	Percentage return on investment
Site only	260	44	16.92
1 house	410	110	26.83
2 houses	560	330	58.93
3 houses	710	800	112.68
4 houses	860	975	113.37
Hotel	1010	1150	113.86

PICCADILLY

	Cumulative development cost £	Rent £	Percentage return on investment
Site only	280	44	17.14
1 house	430	120	27.91
2 houses	580	360	62.07
3 houses	730	850	116.44
4 houses	880	1025	116.48
Hotel	1030	1200	116.51

	Regent Street	Oxford Street	Bond Street
Purchase price	£300	£300	£320
Basic rent	£26	£26	£28

	Houses cost £200 each Hotels cost £1000 each (£200 plus 4 houses)		

REGENT STREET and OXFORD STREET

	Cumulative development cost £	Rent £	Percentage return on investment
Site only	300	52	17.33
1 house	500	130	26.0
2 houses	700	390	55.71
3 houses	900	900	100.0
4 houses	1100	1100	100.0
Hotel	1300	1275	98.08

BOND STREET

	Cumulative development cost £	Rent £	Percentage return on investment
Site only	320	56	17.50
1 house	520	150	28.85
2 houses	720	450	62.50
3 houses	920	1000	108.70
4 houses	1120	1200	107.14
Hotel	1320	1400	106.06

PROPERTY DEVELOPMENT STRATEGY
Dark Blue Property Group

	Park Lane	Mayfair
Purchase price	£350	£400
Basic rent	£35	£50

	Houses cost £200 each Hotels cost £1000 each (£200 plus 4 houses)

PARK LANE

	Cumulative development cost £	Rent £	Percentage return on investment
Site only	350	70	20.0
1 house	550	175	31.82
2 houses	750	500	66.67
3 houses	950	1100	115.79
4 houses	1150	1300	113.04
Hotel	1350	1500	111.11

MAYFAIR

	Cumulative development cost £	Rent £	Percentage return on investment
Site only	400	100	25.0
1 house	600	200	33.33
2 houses	800	600	75.0
3 houses	1000	1400	140.0
4 houses	1200	1700	141.67
Hotel	1400	2000	142.86

PROPERTY DEVELOPMENT STRATEGY
The Three House Rule

If you examine the Property Development Tables you will notice that when you are developing a property group the biggest increase in rental always occurs when you erect the third house on a property. This is true for every colour group.

The 'Three House Rule' is one of the most important factors to bear in mind when developing property groups. To show how important it is, let's see it in large type:

FOR OPTIMUM INVESTMENT AIM FOR THREE HOUSES ON EACH SITE AS FAST AS YOU CAN

PROPERTY DEVELOPMENT STRATEGY
Which Property Group should you develop First?

If you own only one property group, you have very little choice. You must go all out to build three houses on each site of your colour group.

If you own two or more complete colour groups, then you must decide which is the most profitable group to develop first. You will find that it is nearly always better to develop the less expensive properties first. This is simply because for a given amount of money you can buy more houses for an inexpensive group than you can buy for an expensive group. And the return on your investment is comparatively much better for several houses on each lot of a low-cost colour group than for fewer houses on a high-cost colour group.

Here are some examples:

OUTLAY OF £450
= THREE HOUSES PER LIGHT BLUE PROPERTY
= ONE HOUSE PER YELLOW PROPERTY

	Rent for unimproved sites	Rent for developed property	Increase in rent
Light blue	£12 or £16	£270 or £300	£258 or £284
Yellow	£44	£110 or £120	£66 or £76

PROPERTY DEVELOPMENT STRATEGY
Which Property Group should you develop First?

OUTLAY OF £600
= TWO HOUSES PER ORANGE PROPERTY
= ONE HOUSE PER GREEN PROPERTY

	Rent for unimproved sites	Rent for developed property	Increase in rent
Orange	£28 or £32	£200 or £220	£172 or £188
Green	£52 or £56	£130 or £150	£78 or £94

The light blue group and the orange group give the best return. Develop one of these groups first if you own them. Remember also that these two groups include properties that have a better-than-average chance of being landed on. If you do not own either of these groups, it is worth developing either the crimson or the brown group before developing more expensive property groups.

No matter which group you choose to develop first, you should remember the Three House Rule: 'For optimum

The Elephant Query

They say an elephant never forgets, but what's he got to remember?

The Monopoly Answer

If he wants to win, the Three House Rule

PROPERTY DEVELOPMENT STRATEGY
Which Property Group should you develop First?

investment aim for three houses on each site as fast as you can.'

When you have three houses on each property of your first group, leave it there and start developing another group. The rental income from your first group will enable you to develop your second, more expensive group more quickly.

PROPERTY DEVELOPMENT STRATEGY
The Building Formation

The rules of the game say that you must build evenly on all
the properties of a colour group. If you buy three houses for
the orange group, for instance, you must put one house on
each site. But suppose you can only afford to buy one house
– which site should you put it on? If you can afford two
houses, where should they go?

To answer these questions you must consider two points:
1   The rent is always greater for the property within the
    group that is farthest from GO when compared with the
    other sites in the group with the same number of houses.
2   One property in a group may be landed on more often
    than the others.

The table that follows shows the order in which houses
should be built on the sites in each colour group.

	First	Second	Third
Brown	Whitechapel Road	Old Kent Road	—
Light Blue	PentonvilleRoad	Euston Road	The Angel
Crimson	Northumberland Avenue	Pall Mall	Whitehall
Orange	Vine Street	Marlborough Street	Bow Street
Red	Trafalgar Square	Fleet Street	Strand
Yellow	Piccadilly	Leicester Square	Coventry Street
Green	Bond Street	Regent Street	Oxford Street
Dark Blue	Mayfair	Park Lane	—

PROPERTY DEVELOPMENT STRATEGY
How to Exploit a Building Shortage

When you are developing your properties, you should always keep a watchful eye on the number of houses the Bank has available to sell. If the Bank's supply of houses is running low it is worth making a special effort to buy without delay as many houses as you can possibly afford.

If you follow the 'Three House Rule' you will erect three houses on each site of every colour group you own before you consider developing any property further. When you have reached this stage you may set your sights on hotels. It is true that erecting a hotel on a building site enables you to collect the maximum rent, but when there is any chance of a building shortage it is often more advantageous to stick at four houses. That way you monopolize the supply of houses and prevent your opponents from developing their properties any further. (This monopoly of the houses is the feature that gives the game its name.)

If you already own hotels and any of your opponents are still at the stage of development where they have no more than three houses on some sites, you may wish to prevent them from buying any more houses. You may be able to do this by *creating* a housing shortage if you sell some of your hotels back to the Bank in exchange for four houses. You will lose some rent, but this may be preferable to letting your opponents increase their rents by buying more houses.

Renard's Observation

I finally know what distinguishes man from the other beasts: financial worries

HOW TO HANDLE FINANCE

Knowing when to spend your cash and when to hold on to it is one of the most important skills in Monopoly.

Unfortunately it is also one of the most complex.

First let's look at two typical players as examples of how *not* to handle your finances.

Player A is a spendthrift. He does not believe in keeping any cash in reserve. He has spent almost every pound he has in buying property and has erected a few houses on one of his property groups. He lands on another player's property. Since he does not have any cash available he sells some houses back to the Bank to raise the rent that he has to pay. On his next turn he lands on GO and collects £200 salary. As soon as he has the money in his hands he spends it all on buying back the houses he has just sold to the Bank. On his next turn he throws a 1 and a 3, so he lands on Income Tax. So he has to sell his houses back to the Bank again. Then his opponent lands on his property and has to pay him rent, which he immediately uses to buy houses.

The Stevenson Precept

There was a time when a fool and his money were soon parted, but now it happens to everybody

The Brandreth Conundrum

We all know that a fool and his money are soon parted. What we need to know is how they got together in the first place

HOW TO HANDLE FINANCE

And so it goes on. Every time he has to pay out he sells houses. And every time he receives any money he immediately uses it to buy houses again. Since for every house he sells he gets only one half of what he paid for it he is obviously wasting a lot of money by not keeping some cash in reserve.

Player B is a cautious fellow. He owns the orange property group – Bow Street, Marlborough Street and Vine Street. Neither he nor any of his opponents have yet erected any houses. He has £800 in cash but he wants to hold on to this as a reserve. As the game goes on he amasses more and more money and eventually decides that he can afford to erect two houses on each of the orange properties. Meanwhile his opponents have landed on the orange properties several times and have paid him rents of £28 or £32 each time. If he had erected two houses on each property sooner they would instead have been paying him rents of £200 or £220 each time. So his extreme caution has lost him many hundreds of pounds in rental income, which could have been used to buy even more houses and push up the rents even higher.

Now you know how you shouldn't behave, learn these Seven Rules of Financial Security and you should manage to stay solvent.

Dunn's Discovery

The shortest measurable interval of time is the time between the moment I put a little extra cash aside for a sudden emergency and the arrival of that emergency

HOW TO HANDLE FINANCE

1 Before you spend any cash to buy properties or buildings, examine your financial situation carefully.
2 Try to leave yourself enough cash to cover any expenses you might incur in the near future. This includes provision for possible penalties from Chance and Community Chest; taxes; and any rental charges you might incur as a result of landing on properties owned by other players. Try to estimate the probability of these items of expenditure, and budget accordingly.
3 Take into account income that might come to you in the near future.

  Will your token pass GO in the next throw or two, providing you with £200 salary?

  How near are your opponents' tokens to any property that you own? For example, if your opponent's token is on JUST VISITING and you own the crimson and orange property groups with several houses on each property there is a good chance that on his next throw he will land on one of your properties, providing you with rental income. Whereas if his token is on FREE PARKING you cannot anticipate any rental income at all.

  If there is a good probability that your opponent will, on his next throw, land on some property that you are planning to develop, you should be prepared to risk more of your cash reserve to develop that property than you would normally.
4 When assessing your cash reserve, take into account the cash that you can raise, if needed, by mortgaging such properties as single sites which do not form part of a complete colour group, single Railway Stations, and the Utilities if the game is well advanced. If the rental income

HOW TO HANDLE FINANCE

you might lose by mortgaging such properties and the 10 per cent interest you will have to pay to lift the mortgages is small in comparison to the increased rental income you can get from developing other properties then you need have no qualms about mortgaging these less valuable properties.

5   Always try to avoid being placed in a situation where you have to mortgage properties from complete colour groups because your cash reserve was too low.

6   Above all, try to avoid being placed in a situation where you need to sell buildings back to the Bank. That way you lose half the money you have invested in the buildings and you seriously affect your rental-earning capacity.

Woody Allen's Theory

Money is better than poverty, if only for financial reasons

7   Finally, realize when the moment has come to abandon all caution and go for broke. This will be when an opponent has developed his property to such an extent that you are going to be wiped out if you land on it. It may be that you will be bankrupt or, at least, be forced to sell so many buildings and mortgage so much property to pay the high rent that you might as well resign.

In this situation the best strategy is to pick one of your complete colour groups and develop it as quickly as you can; mortgage or sell everything else you own; and spend every last pound buying buildings to erect on your

HOW TO HANDLE FINANCE

selected property group. That done, all you can do is pray for your opponent to land on your property before you land on his.

Brandreth's Rule of Desperation

When accidentally spilling hot coffee all over the Monopoly board ensure that the accident occurs *before* your opponents realize that you are about to go bankrupt

AUCTION STRATEGY

When you bid for a property that is being sold by auction you'll do so for one of three reasons:

1 Because you want the property.
2 Because you want to prevent another player from getting it.
3 Because you want to force up the bidding so that the player who buys the property will have paid more than if you had not intervened.

AUCTION STRATEGY
Bidding for Property You Want

If the property being sold is one that you want you must be prepared to outbid your opponents. Before the bidding starts it is a wise move to set yourself a limit. This will prevent you from being carried away by the excitement of the auction and bidding more than you can possibly afford or more than the property is really worth to you. When deciding the limit you will go to, ask yourself how much you actually need the property that is being sold. Then review your cash situation, and what you can mortgage or sell, if necessary, to raise extra cash.

AUCTION STRATEGY
Bidding to Stop an Opponent

If your aim is merely to prevent an opponent from obtaining the property, this is usually because it will provide him with a complete property group. But there may be other players who are just as concerned as you are to prevent that opponent from acquiring the property. Make sure that they appreciate the seriousness of the situation, and get them to bid against him. If you're lucky, one of them will be successful, and your objective will have been achieved at their expense rather than your own.

AUCTION STRATEGY
Forcing up the Bidding

If you enter an auction, not with the intention of buying the property, but merely to force up the bidding, be very, very careful. When this strategy works it is a neat way of depleting your opponent's funds. But if you are unsuccessful you will wind up paying a lot of money for a property you don't need.

Donohue's Dictum

What's worth doing is worth doing for money

The Successful Trader's Maxim

You can fool some of the people all of the time and all of the people some of the time – a combination of which will win you the game

SUCCESSFUL TRADING

Private trading between players is one of the most important aspects of Monopoly.

The nature of the game can vary a good deal, depending on the number of players. When there are only two players, the game usually develops in one of two ways:

1 One player gets one or more complete property groups, and the other player gets none. Nothing but a miracle will prevent the player with the complete property groups from winning.

2 Both players get one or more complete property groups. In this case the result will depend on which player develops his properties first, or on which player lands on his opponent's properties most often.

In either of these situations a game may well be played to the finish without any trading taking place at all. Occasionally, however, in a two-player game there will be a situation where neither player manages to land on and acquire a complete property group. When this happens, the players must trade properties with each other so that both players get complete groups. Unless this trade takes place, the game is likely to go on forever, with neither player being able to force the other into submission.

When there are more players, trading is much more common. Indeed, when there are a large number of players, this is often the only way any player can acquire a complete property group.

Successful trading is an important skill – which has to be learnt if you want to succeed in Monopoly.

SUCCESSFUL TRADING
Mutual Deals

The commonest kind of deal is between two players, when each player has a property that is required by the other to complete a colour group. For instance:

Player A owns Pall Mall and Whitehall   (crimson)
         and Vine Street   (orange)
Player B owns Northumberland Avenue   (crimson)
         and Bow Street and Marlborough Street   (orange)

Suppose you are Player A – would you trade Vine Street for Northumberland Avenue?

The answer must depend on the circumstances. If Player B has plenty of cash and you have very little, the deal would *not* be favourable to you. He could immediately spend all his cash on houses for the orange properties. If you land on one of them you could be in deep trouble.

So, in general, you should only consider a deal of this sort if you can develop the property group you acquire before your opponent can develop the property group he acquires.

What about the terms of the deal? Player A could argue: 'I'm giving you Vine Street, which is worth £200, and you're giving me Northumberland Avenue which is only worth £160 – so you'll also have to give me £40 in cash to make the deal square.' On the other hand, player B could argue: 'The values of the properties don't matter. You *need* Northumberland just as much I need Vine Street – so we ought to do a straight swap.' Player B might even be able to argue: 'You need this trade if you're going to have a chance of staying in the game. Unless *you* give *me* £100 the deal is off!'

This argument could become complicated, with bluff and double-bluff entering into it. Who will win the argument depends not only on who is the sharpest trader but also on the circumstances of the game.

SUCCESSFUL TRADING
Cash Sales

Another type of deal is where one player who has plenty of money buys a property from another player.

The player who is selling the property usually does so for one of two reasons:

1   His financial situation is very bad. Perhaps he needs the cash to pay his debts.
2   He is disposing of a property he does not require in order to raise the cash to develop a complete property group.

The buyer, likewise, usually has one of two reasons for wishing to buy the property:

1   Because it will help him to complete a property group.
2   To stop the property going to another player, who needs it to complete a property group.

If you are the seller in a deal like this, first offer the property to the player who needs it to complete a colour group. Then see if you can get a better offer from another player in whose interest it is to stop the first player buying it. Even if this ploy is unsuccessful, it is usually better to sell to the player who does not need the property rather than to the player who does – though it may mean accepting a lower price.

Iron Law of Distribution

Them what has – gets

SUCCESSFUL TRADING
Multilateral Deals

Suppose Player A has a property you want and he is willing to let it go, but you don't have anything he will accept in exchange. However, you do own a property that is wanted by Player B, and he has a property that player A requires.

This is where the multilateral deal comes in. You first negotiate a deal with player B, whereby you get the property required by Player A. You then let Player A have this property in exchange for the property you want.

This way you manage to obtain the property you want, and everyone is happy. If you are sufficiently astute, you can ensure that you also make a nice profit on the deal. That's the reward for being the middleman.

If you want to trade wisely and well try remembering Brandreth's Three Tips for Traders:
1 In your deals, always try to make absolutely sure that the benefits you get outweigh the benefits given to the other player.
2 Look for imaginative deals. For example, imagine this scenario:

You own	Regent Street and Oxford Street	(Green)
	Strand	(Red)
Player A owns	Bond Street	(Green)
	Fleet Street and Trafalgar Square	(Red)

Your first thought might be to offer Player A Strand in exchange for Bond Street. But hold on a minute. The reds are nearly always a better property group to own than the greens. You'll be giving an advantage to your opponent.

Why not offer Player A your two greens in exchange

SUCCESSFUL TRADING
Multilateral Deals

for his two reds? Tell Player A that you're doing him a great favour – it's just that red is your favourite colour. You'll probably also persuade him to part with several hundred pounds for letting him have the more expensive properties.

3 Look at the properties held by the other players. Try to foresee where they might be able to trade between themselves to your disadvantage. Try to forestall such deals by doing a trade, yourself, with either one of them.

Emerson's Observation

It requires a great deal of boldness and a great deal of caution to make a great fortune, and when you have got it, it requires ten times as much wit to keep it

MORTGAGE WISELY AND WELL

Mortgaging is the only permitted way of borrowing from the Bank, and it is a useful way of raising money. Many inexperienced players regard mortgaging as something to be avoided – something you have to do to pay your debts if you have no other option. But there is more to mortgages than that. Mortgaging can be employed creatively. When, for example, you own a complete property group it is often a good idea to mortgage other properties in order to raise the money to develop this property group as quickly as possible.

Aesop's Law of Exploitation
Wealth unused might as well not exist

First consider the cost of mortgaging. This cost is twofold:

1   The 10 per cent interest that you must pay when eventually you decide to lift the mortgage. This is seldom a very important consideration. For instance, the mortgage value of Mayfair – which is the most expensive property on the board – is £200, so the interest cost of a mortgage is *at most* £20.

2   The other element in the cost of a mortgage is the potential loss of rental income. This is more important than the 10 per cent interest. Therefore when deciding which property to mortgage you should take into account both the amount of rent you may lose and the probability of that property being landed on. Then if you are using the money you raise by mortgaging to develop some other property you should compare the increased rent you are going to get from the property you are

MORTGAGE WISELY AND WELL

developing and the probability of *that* property being landed on.

If you decide to raise money by mortgaging you have to choose which properties you are going to mortgage and in which order. Generally you should mortgage properties in the following order:

1 *Single Building Sites.* If you have a single building site such as Marlborough Street, Piccadilly or Bond Street, and there is no immediate prospect of acquiring the other sites to complete the colour group, this should be the first candidate to be considered for mortgage. Bear in mind that some properties are landed on more frequently than others. If, for example, you have a choice between mortgaging Trafalgar Square or Piccadilly, you should mortgage Piccadilly.

2 *Utilities.* If you own either the Water Works or the Electric Company, but not both, this can be mortgaged without too much loss. If you own both, however, remember that they are very worthwhile properties to own early in the game but of much less value later on. So try not to mortgage them until the game is fairly well advanced and rents are beginning to be reckoned in hundreds of pounds instead of being reckoned in tens of pounds.

3 *Single Railway Stations.* If you can own only one Railway Station this should be considered as a good property to mortgage – especially if it is Liverpool Street, which is landed on much less frequently than the other Railway Stations.

4 *Pairs of Building Sites.* If you own two out of three sites of a colour group and the third site is still held by the Bank, avoid mortgaging either of these sites if you can. If the

MORTGAGE WISELY AND WELL

third site is owned by one of your opponents, is there any possibility of being able to do a trade with him so you can get this site to complete your colour group? If so, try not to mortgage the two lots you already own. If there is no possibility of completing the colour group regard the two sites you own as mortgageable.

5   *Two or more Railway Stations.* If you own two or more Railway Stations you must consider what stage the game is at. If there is not much property development on the board the rental income you get from your Railway Stations – £50 from each Railway Station if you own two, £100 if you own three, and £200 if you own all four – is quite advantageous. At this stage of the game you should try to avoid mortgaging your Railway Stations. Later in the game the rent from your Railway Stations might seem small in comparison to the rent for highly developed properties, and you might then consider mortgaging them, especially if you are going to use the cash to buy more houses to get even higher rents for your complete property groups.

6   *Complete property groups.* You should consider mortgaging these only as a last resort when you need the money to pay debts and you have no other option open to you. This is especially true when you have erected buildings on any of the properties of a colour group. Remember that before you can mortgage any property of a colour group you must sell any buildings on that colour group back to the Bank for one half of their value.

When you consider mortgaging any property bear in mind the positions of your opponents' tokens. If any of your opponents is likely to land on the property in his next turn or

MORTGAGE WISELY AND WELL

two you should wait, if you can, until he has either landed on the property or gone past it before you mortgage it.

Huxley's Cash Conundrum

The size of sums of money appears to vary remarkably according as they are being paid in or paid out

The Monopoly Corollary

It's more fun getting rent than paying it

HOW LONG SHOULD YOU STAY IN JAIL?

If you get sent to Jail – as you usually will, several times in the course of a game – should you pay to get out on your very next turn or should you stay in Jail for the maximum of three turns in the hope of throwing a double and getting out free, thus saving £50?

Generally the answer to this question depends on the stage the game has reached.

Newton's Little-known Seventh Law

A bird in the hand is safer than two overhead

The Monopoly Corollary

If the game's nearly over and you land in Jail – stay there

In the early stages of the game you should always choose to get out of Jail on the first throw, either by using a 'Get Out of Jail Free' card if you have one or by paying the £50 fine. At this stage of the game there are still plenty of unowned properties on the board and nobody will yet have acquired a complete property group or started building. Being stuck in jail is definitely a disadvantage. You ought to be out there moving round the board, landing on unowned property and buying it, not letting your opponents do all the property-buying. Any rent you might incur by landing on property owned by other players at this early stage in the game is likely to be an irritation rather than a major setback.

Later in the game – when there is no unowned property left and houses and hotels are springing up – being in Jail can

HOW LONG SHOULD YOU STAY IN JAIL?

be a real advantage and you should aim to stay there as long as you can. Remember that while you are in Jail you can continue trading, buying and selling, mortgaging, *and collecting rent*. While you are behind bars you are not going to be paying any rent to your opponents whereas they are moving round the board and, hopefully, landing on your properties and paying rent to you.

In between the two extremes it may be more difficult to decide whether it is better to stay in Jail or to get out as quickly as possible. Here are the questions you should ask yourself to help you decide:

1   What is your cash position? Is the payment of the £50 fine going to hurt you so much that it is worth hanging on in there with the hope that you might throw doubles and thus get out free? Bear in mind that while you are in Jail you are not moving round the board towards GO and that £200 salary.

2   How many unowned properties are there left? Are there any that you need to buy to get a complete colour group? Or any that you need to buy to stop your opponents from getting complete colour groups? Can you afford to stay in Jail while your opponents move round the board and possibly snap up those properties?

3   Do your opponents have building developments with high rents making it unwise to venture out of the safety of Jail before you need to?

GAMESMANSHIP

Gamesmanship is defined as the art of winning games, without actually cheating, by disconcerting, confusing or misleading your opponents.

Canada Bill Jones's Motto

It is morally wrong to allow suckers to keep their money

The Monopoly Corollary

Even if God isn't a capitalist, be sure you're playing suckers and your victory will be morally acceptable

The three ploys that follow on pages 158–61 are particular favourites of mine and are quite legitimate.

GAMESMANSHIP
The Hidden Assets Ploy

There are times when it is important to know how much cash an opponent has. This is especially true when you are trading with him. Conversely, it is equally important for him to know how much cash you have.

Suppose you are considering a trade which will result in your opponent owning the complete yellow group of properties and you owning the complete crimson property group. Suppose also that you have enough cash to erect one house on each of the crimson properties but he has so much cash that he could immediately erect three houses on each of the yellow properties. As a result of this deal he would own a property group with rents of £800, £800 and £850, whereas the rents on your properties would be a paltry £50, £50 and £60. You would quite rightly turn this deal down flat.

If, on the other hand, he has very little cash he will not be able to erect any houses on the yellow properties immediately. So his rents will only be £44, £44 and £48. And it will probably be a long time before he can afford the £450 it

The Panicked Player's Paradox

The objective of all dedicated Monopoly players should be to analyse thoroughly all situations, anticipate all problems prior to their occurrence, concentrate at all times and never for a second be anything other than cool, calm, clear-headed and cunningly calculating. However, when you are up to your neck in alligators, it is difficult to remind yourself that your initial objective was to drain the swamp

GAMESMANSHIP
The Hidden Assets Ploy

will cost to erect even one house on each of the properties. In this case the trade will probably be a very good one for you to make.

For you to make the right decision on a trade like this, you need to know how much cash your opponent has. For him to make the right decision, he will need to know how much cash *you* have. So it will be to your advantage if he thinks you have less cash than you really do have.

The rules say that your Title Deed cards should be clearly displayed so that your opponents can see which properties you own. But the rules say nothing about displaying your cash. So why not keep a few of your £100 or £500 notes discreetly out of sight – tucked under that pile of £1 notes, perhaps – and bluff your opponents into thinking you are poorer than you really are? In championship play, players need not disclose how much money they have, but the money must be kept in full view on the table at all times. The money may be stacked in any order of the players' choosing.

Wilson's Pipe Ploy

Even if you don't smoke, play the game with a pipe in your hand. A pipe gives a wise man time to think and a fool something to stick in his mouth

GAMESMANSHIP
The Opponents' Rent Ploy

When a player's token lands on property owned by another player, it is the owner's responsibility to point this out and demand the rent. If he fails to do so before the next player throws the dice he can not claim any rent.

Although it is not part of the official rules, many players adopt the rule that you may not help another player to watch out for rents that are due to him.

This rule, however, may easily be sidestepped. Suppose one of your opponents owns Park Lane and it has just been landed on by another of your opponents. The owner does not notice and does not claim any rent. Before the next player throws the dice, you cry out, 'Park Lane! I think I own that! You'll have to pay me some rent.' You look over your Title Deeds and then say with a look of surprise, 'I'm sorry, I don't own Park Lane. I thought I did.' Unless the real owner of Park Lane has fallen asleep he will realize that he owns it and will claim his rent. But you haven't helped him, have you? You just made an innocent mistake!

Naturally, you will only make use of this ploy very occasionally, and only when it is to your advantage to do so. That is when the player who has to pay the rent is more of a threat to you than the player to whom the rent is due. In the situation where the player who has neglected to claim his rent is a greater threat to you, you sit tight and gloat silently.

GAMESMANSHIP
The Disinterested Bidding Ploy

Gamesmanship is essential when you are bidding for a property you want to acquire when it is put up for auction. You must always try to appear casual, as if you couldn't be bothered whether you get the property or not. Never, never show that you are keen to get the property.

If you show that you are anxious to get the property your opponents will bid more highly just to thwart your plans. But if you use this ploy successfully and convince your opponents that you are really disinterested you stand a chance of getting the property cheaply.

Sophocles' Plea for Fair Play

I would prefer to fail with honour than win by cheating

Brandreth's Sophoclean Observation

Sophocles may not have been a cheat, but he was obviously a liar

THE CHEAT'S STRATEGY

Ten tricks no gentleman (male or female) would dream of stooping to in a mean attempt to disconcert and distract the other players.

1. Have a violent attack of the hiccups during all turns except your own.

2. Hum softly, tunelessly, constantly.

3. Pick your teeth with the 'Get Out Of Jail Free' card.

4. Raise an eyebrow and chuckle smugly at the end of an opponent's move.

5. As soon as an opponent's turn begins start to drum your fingers on the table and mutter, 'Come on! Come on! We haven't got all day.'

6. Keep up a constant flow of chatter – and make it relevant. For example, why not *name* every house that's erected on the board: 'I think that house of yours on Vine Street should be called the Titanic, because of the rising damp, and let's call this one here on Park Lane the Marie Celeste, because no one's in when the bailiffs call!'

7. Keep up a constant flow chatter – and make it irrelevant. 'Did you know that butter melts at 88°F and that the Kampuchean alphabet has seventy-two letters? I bet you didn't know that my mother once met Clint Eastwood. It was in New York in 1982, when she was on holiday . . .'

THE CHEAT'S STRATEGY

8 If you are playing with pounds refer to them as dollars or pesetas or yen – or anything at all except pounds.

9 Yawn loudly and repeatedly. Yawning is catching so it won't be long before all your opponents are yawning too, when you must ask them sharply to kindly cease yawning and get on with the game or concede defeat and go to bed.

10 Extol the virtues of Scrabble.

Part Four

MONOPOLY MISCELLANY

or
'There's more than one way to skin
a cat'

THE JOB REPORT

A survey of the occupations of competitors entering Monopoly championships in Britain, the USA, Canada and Australia, suggests that your success as a player may depend on your professional background.

The most successful Monopoly players tend to be:

1 Merchant bankers
2 Bankers
3 Accountants
4 Students
5 Computer programmers
6 Systems analysts
7 Lawyers
8 Architects
9 Professional gamblers
10 Airline pilots

In the international league table estate agents come eleventh.

The Variety Dilemma

Variety is the spice of life – unless you don't happen to like change, in which case you probably don't like spice either

---

THE JOB REPORT

The least successful players tend to be:
1. Teachers
2. Entertainers
3. Doctors
4. Truck drivers
5. Artists

Why is it that students are among the most successful players while teachers are among the least successful? Students, of course, have time to practise – but so do teachers. This suggests either that practice doesn't make perfect after all or that this survey is quite as unreliable as every other survey produced since the dawn of civilization.

Women in Monopoly

In Monopoly Championships around the world women have competed half as often as men yet been successful twice as often. This is a statistical truth, so if you want to win the game make sure you're a woman and your opponents are all men. Unluckily, this can be difficult

---

MONOPOLY VARIATIONS

The game of Monopoly has been in existence for half a century now. Inevitably in that time a host of variations of the standard game have come into existence.

Some of the variations are very local – a family, perhaps, adapting the rules to suit themselves – or simply misunderstanding them or misinterpreting them. I have known families who played the game incorrectly for years, never imagining there was any other way of playing but their own.

A number of variations have become established, and are widely recognized as alternatives to the standard game.

I don't like any of them much, but you may, so here they are.

MONOPOLY VARIATIONS
Short Game

One variation of Monopoly for a short game is described in Waddingtons' official rules (see Appendix).

Monopoly – The Facts

In Charles Darrow's original version of the rules of the game, there was no Short Game. Parker Brothers insisted on including the alternative because they had never previously marketed a game with an indefinite playing time

---

MONOPOLY VARIATIONS
The Go Variation

In the normal game a player collects £200 salary whenever he lands on or passes GO. In this variation a player still collects £200 if he *passes* GO, but if actually *lands on* GO he is rewarded with a double salary of £400.

MONOPOLY VARIATIONS
The Free Parking Jackpot

Before the game starts the Banker places a £500 note under the FREE PARKING space. In the course of the game players who have to pay fines or taxes add that money to the FREE PARKING pot instead of paying it to the Bank. (When purchasing properties or buildings, players pay the money to the Bank, as in the normal game).

Whenever a player *lands on* FREE PARKING he collects whatever is in the pot at that time. The first player to land on FREE PARKING is in luck because he collects the £500 placed there by the Bank plus whatever has been added by the players. The Bank, after its initial bout of generosity, does not put any more money in the pot. So any players landing on FREE PARKING subsequently collect only what the players have put in the pot since FREE PARKING was last landed on.

MONOPOLY VARIATIONS
Maximum Punishment

In the standard game a player who is in Jail may still buy or sell property, buy or sell houses, mortgage property or lift mortgages, trade with other players, and collect rents.

In the Maximun Punishment variation, a player forfeits all these rights during the time he spends in Jail.

MONOPOLY VARIATIONS
Best of Three

This variation of Monopoly is designed to increase the skill element by giving players an opportunity to choose which space they will land on when they throw the dice.

The distinguishing feature of this variation is that each player, when it is his turn, throws *three* dice. He may then ignore any one of the dice, and only the other two values count towards his score.

A few examples will demonstrate how this works.

Values shown by dice	Effective throw
2, 3, 4	5 or 6 or 7
3, 5, 6	8 or 9 or 11
1, 1, 4	2 (doubles) or 5
4, 4, 4	8 (doubles)

This variation usually takes much longer to play than the normal game as it is easier to avoid landing on property owned by another player. The key to success is to own long stretches of properties next to one another, so that there is less chance of them being passed over.

The Law of Monopoly Variations

No one ever suggests playing a Monopoly variation when they have just won the game playing with the standard rules. Only unsuccessful Monopoly players regularly use the variations and the more unsuccessful they are the more variations they try

ODDBALL GAMES

One of the crazier manifestations of man's innate competitive instinct is the desire to establish new Monopoly records.

So widespread is this desire that it was deemed necessary to establish a committee to adjudicate on and record marathon records in various categories. This group, organized by Parker Brothers in Salem, Massachusetts, goes under the bewitching title of the Monopoly Marathon Records Documentation Committee.

ODDBALL GAMES
Two-player Longest Game Record

The longest session between two players was held at the Power House Youth Club in Birmingham, England in May 1972 when Eric Foxall and Gary Davies played for 86 hours.

Also in 1972, however, the Monopoly Marathon Records Documentation Committee, after consulting several distinguished physicians, decided that they would no longer accept or do anything to encourage marathon attempts in this category because of the hazard to the health of the participants.

ODDBALL GAMES
Marathons Unlimited

A Monopoly marathon, as it is now accepted, may involve an unlimited number of players, playing a consecutive series of games. As soon as one game ends the next must begin.

In July 1971 a group of people in Danville, California, played in a non-stop Monopoly marathon that lasted 820 hours. Twenty people took part. They started at noon on July 21 and played continuously for thirty-four days, finishing at 4 p.m. on August 24.

Three years later, in 1974, this record was beaten in Denver, Colorado. Thirty-four students, playing in two-player, four-hour relays, staged their marathon in a Denver department store. Starting at noon on June 18 they played until noon on July 30 – a total of 1008 hours non-stop play.

But this record did not stand very long. In March 1976 a group of sixty students of Georgia Technical College in Atlanta played continuously for 1176 hours.

The current record holders are the McCluer North Games Club in Florissant, Missouri, who played for 1416 hours (59 days).

ODDBALL GAMES
Biggest, Deepest, Highest

Other records have been established for playing Monopoly in the most unusual circumstances.

The record for playing Monopoly underground was set in 1974 by eight teenagers in Greeley, Colorado. They played in a hole measuring 10 feet by 4 feet by 4 feet, which two of the boys had dug in their back yard. Their underground marathon lasted 100 hours. They were suitably rewarded with a huge cake decorated as an exact replica of a Monopoly board.

For the longest anti-gravity game the board was drawn on the ceiling of the players' room and, using helium-filled balloons, they managed to play for 36 hours.

The largest outdoor game of Monopoly (550 ft × 470 ft) was played in 1967 by students from Juniata College in Huntington, Pennsylvania. Actual campus streets were used, the dice were large foam rubber cubes thrown from a third floor fire escape, the tokens were people, and the players used walkie-talkies to relay their moves to one another.

In London there has also been a life-size game using the actual streets corresponding to those on the Monopoly board. The players, a group of Boy Scouts from Chelmsford, moved from one location to another according to the throw of the dice using whatever means of transport were available – bus, underground or on foot. GO was the Scout Headquarters in the centre of London. Players who landed on GO had to report there. Players passing GO were paid the cost of a phone call in addition to their salary, so they could phone in to report their positions.

One of the most popular forms of playing Monopoly, however, appears to be underwater. The record for this is

ODDBALL GAMES
Biggest, Deepest, Highest

held by the Buffalo (NY) Dive Club when in 1983, 350 divers in wet suits played in relays for 1080 hours of non-stop play.

The first attempt at this record back in 1967 set Parker Brothers a bit of a problem – how to stop the board and money from disintegrating in the water and how to stop the playing pieces from floating to the surface. The attempt was being made by a group of divers from New England Divers Inc. in Beverly, Massachusetts, and they called on Parker Brothers to see what they could come up with. Parker Brothers' engineers worked for three weeks and finally emerged with a board which weighed 95 pounds. The board was backed with a steel plate and laminated with cellophane. The houses and hotels were filled with steel wool. The Title Deed, Community Chest and Chance cards were sandwiched with metal and laminated in cellophane, thus producing a game which was both waterproof and submersible. According to Parker Brothers, they lend out this set so often that it barely has time to get dry between games.

In the UK, Waddingtons have also been called on to produce their own version of sub-aqua Monopoly.

ODDBALL GAMES
The Richest Game

In November 1973 an exhibition game was held, using real US currency instead of Monopoly money. The game took place in the Manhattan Savings Bank, which also provided the cash. Russell Smith, the bank's chairman, acted – appropriately – as Banker for the game. At one point the Monopoly bank ran out of funds, and extra cash had to be fetched from the vaults of the Savings Bank. All funds were returned when the game was over!

During the UK championship final in September 1984 real money was also used.

WORLD MONOPOLY MARATHON RECORDS

Official categories	Current record
Longest game with unlimited number of players	1416 hours (59 days)
Longest game with five players	624 hours (26 days)
Longest game with four players	660 hours (27 days, 12 hours)
Longest game with three players	286 hours (11 days, 22 hours)
Longest game played in a tree house	240 hours (10 days)
Longest game played in a moving lift	384 hours (16 days)
Longest game played underground (record no longer kept for safety reasons)	100 hours (4 days, 4 hours)
Longest game played in a bath (minimum six inches of water)	99 hours (4 days, 3 hours)
Longest game played on a balance beam (safety mats required)	200 hours (8 days, 8 hours)
Longest anti-gravity (upside down) game	36 hours (played on a ceiling)
Longest game played underwater	1080 hours (45 days)

WORLD MONOPOLY MARATHON RECORDS

Official categories	Current record
Longest game played on the back of a fire engine	101 hours (4 days, 5 hours)
Largest outdoor game	550 ft × 470 ft
Largest indoor game	122 ft × 122 ft
Smallest game (1 inch square)	30 hours

Franklin's Law

Blessed is he who expects nothing, for he shall not be disappointed

The Monopoly Corollary

If you want not to lose more than you want to win, you'll end up simply wanting

MONOPOLY CHAMPIONSHIPS

To mark Monopoly's 40th anniversary in 1975, Parker Brothers decided to organize a World Tournament, and championships have been held ever since every two or three years. The various overseas licensees, in places as far away as Japan, South Africa and Peru, hold their own regional championships prior to the world event, and the winner then goes on to compete for the World title the following year. The British Championships, which usually take the form of regional heats culminating in a Grand Final, are organized by Waddingtons.

The idea for a British Championship had actually first taken root in 1973. In that year two London property men, Bill Smith and Brian Nuttall, who ran Mithras Properties and who also happened to be Monopoly enthusiasts, thought that it would be 'a bit of a giggle' to find the best Monopoly players in the City. The Mithras Property Monopoly Championship of Great Britain was born. Waddingtons were called in to officiate as entries poured in from merchant bankers, property men, stockbrokers, insurance agents and estate agents to take part in the 92 two-men-team contest held in the Savoy Hotel, London. So successful was the competition that another was organized in the following year, raising many thousands of pounds for charity.

When Parker Brothers announced that they were to hold the first World Championship in 1975, Waddingtons set to work to find a British Champion. After some initial reluctance from the authorities, they persuaded British Rail to allow them to set up their 40 tables and 240 chairs on platforms 3 and 4 of Fenchurch Street station. The contest went surprisingly smoothly considering that trains continued to arrive every twenty minutes, disgorging their

MONOPOLY CHAMPIONSHIPS

passengers on to what was already an overcrowded platform. At one table a player went bankrupt only eight minutes after the game had started! On another table the aspirations of five smartly dressed city gents were demolished by a nine-year-old competitor, while on yet another table an entrant actually managed to acquire every property on the board! Two further rounds whittled the contestants down to four finalists. Ken Jones, a local government officer from Bolton, got off to an ingenious start by buying the five cheapest properties on the board and quickly buying four houses for each of them. By so doing he had acquired 60 per cent of the housing stock and prevented the others from developing their properties to the extent they would have liked. The strategy paid off, and Ken emerged as the Champion. His prize: a trophy and a polished glass Monopoly table as well as the opportunity to go to the European Championship in Reykjavik, Iceland and then on to the World Championship in Washington DC.

On 18 November 1974 would-be Monopoly Champions from all over Europe descended on Reykjavik to do battle for the European title. The elegant Crystal Room of the Loftleidir Hotel was the venue. The organizers left no stone unturned to make this a memorable event; from the specially chartered plane, which was to take all the winners on to the USA four days later, the special sightseeing tours, the cocktail parties and the razzmatazz of the championship itself. Then came the moment everyone had been waiting for. The Crystal Room positively hummed with excitement. The competitors were all seated at their tables with their 'I Love Monopoly' badges and Monopoly mugs specially produced as personal mementoes of the event. Cameras were clicking, flash bulbs

MONOPOLY CHAMPIONSHIPS

were popping. Tension mounted. Then the whistle sounded and the race was on for the 24 competitors. After several hours of ruthless play, the winner was decided: Pierre Milet of France.

Then the competitors were off again to Washington and the World Championship. Here they were joined by the champions from Canada and the USA in the ballroom of the plushy L'Enfant Plaza Hotel where the contest was to take place. The four who made it through to the final round were: Roger Hendricks of Belgium, Cato Wallo of Norway, Ken Jones of Great Britain and John Mair, a merchant banker from Dublin. Despite a rather ignominious entrance – he tripped over a television cable – and although at one stage he mistook his gin and tonic for the dice shaker, John Mair eventually bankrupted his opponents and carried off the title. It turned out that he was not in such a state of inebriation as his opponents assumed him to be, though at the press conference afterwards he attributed his success to 'judgement, genius and gin and tonic'.

The second World Championship was held in Monaco. A couple of months earlier Waddingtons had held the British Championships in an unusual venue – on top of the atomic pile at Oldbury-on-Severn power station (Waddingtons' interpretation of the 'Electric Company'). It was quite safe, although everyone involved had to wear protective clothing and special overshoes and had to carry a personal geiger counter as a radiation safety tester. The winner was Fred Brown, a 34-year-old draughtsman from Southampton.

Once again the British Champion reached the final round of the World Championship, but was beaten into fourth place. John Mair was there to defend his title but he had to be

MONOPOLY CHAMPIONSHIPS

content with second place as 31 year old Chong Seng Kwa, an oil engineer from Singapore, emerged the winner, carrying off the coveted title and a magnificent silver trophy worth $5000.

'Monopoly On The Move' was the theme for the British Championship in 1979. On Thursday 20 September an unusual announcement was heard over the loudspeaker system at Liverpool Street station. 'The next train leaving platform 8 will be the 10.45 Monopoly Express to Kings Cross, calling at Fenchurch Street. All passengers wishing to go to Jail, please take their seats.' Waddingtons had persuaded British Rail to let them use an Inter-City train for the preliminary rounds of the event, but they were not able to obtain permission to use one of HM Prisons for the final round – they settled for the London Dungeon, a museum of horrors in the arches under London Bridge station. The British Champion that year was Simon Wardill, a surveyor with a London firm of estate agents, who received a silver salver and a place in the World Championship in Bermuda.

The 1980 World Championship took place in the Southampton Princess Hotel in Bermuda, and although it was March the temperature was in the 70s. The red-clothed tables were assembled in the brightly-lit hall of the hotel which was ablaze with colour. The prize at stake was indeed worth fighting for: the prestigious title and a trip for two anywhere in the world (valued at $5000). After two days of fierce play, five finalists were eventually announced: Greg Jacobs (Australia), Bernard Lutz (France), Urs Krebs (Switzerland), Dana Terman (USA) and Cesare Bernabei of Italy who finally walked off with the trophy.

The British tournament in 1982 yielded the youngest

MONOPOLY CHAMPIONSHIPS

champion ever – James Mallett, a 12-year-old schoolboy from Gloucester. The contest took place at the magnificent stately home of the Earl and Countess of Bradford at Weston Park, Shifnal, Shropshire. This venue was chosen because, 'Monopoly is about property, and stately homes are probably the epitome of all property in Britain'.

James did well to get through to the final round of the 1983 World Championship the following year. Several factors were against him. He was the youngest contender out of the 26 countries represented. The board, as in all the World Championships, was the unfamiliar American version with Atlantic City street names. But, perhaps more tellingly, he was far from home in the fast-living, high-class surroundings of the millionaires' playground of Palm Beach, Florida. He did however beat the reigning champion, Cesare Bernabei, as well as the German, Swiss, Canadian and Spanish champions to take third place overall. His prize was $1000 in one hundred dollar bills crammed into a top hat, the token with which he had elected to play. The winner that year was Greg Jacobs, an estate agent from Australia, whose prize was $10 000 to spend in a 4-hour shopping spree in Palm Beach's exclusive Worth Avenue – the only time Monopoly money

Monopoly – The Facts

Monopoly was played during the 60-day submersion of a US nuclear submarine under the polar icecap. Special sets have also been made for use by American astronauts on long space missions

MONOPOLY CHAMPIONSHIPS

has been accepted as legal tender.

At the time of writing, the next British Championship is due to take place at the Park Lane Hotel in London where a stoved brass engraved Monopoly set, made by Steve Car of London's Hatton Garden, is used; and the World Championship is planned for the autumn of 1985 – the preliminary rounds being held in New York and the final, appropriately, in Atlantic City itself.

THE MONOPOLY TOKENS

The players' tokens used in a British Monopoly set are a dog, a top hat, a racing car, a boot, an iron and a ship. In Canada, a cowboy, a wheelbarrow, a sports car, a shoe, an iron, a clog, a top hat and a thimble are used, whereas Switzerland uses plastic tokens in the form of a mushroom, a man with a ladder, a four-leaved clover, a pig, a gnome and a ladybird. In Peru they use a dog, a steamship, an oboe, an iron, a racing car, a cannon, a train and a llama. But in Holland, Colombia, Lebanon and Spain, for example, no differentiation is made between the various tokens – all the players use the same type of counter.

MONOPOLY AROUND THE WORLD
Boards used in English Speaking Countries

American	British	Irish	South African
Mediterranean Avenue	Old Kent Road	Crumlin	Musgrave Road/ Musgraveweg
Baltic Avenue	Whitechapel Road	Kimmage	Gillespie Street/ Gillespiestraat
Reading Railroad	Kings Cross	Busaras Dublin	Durban Station/ Durbanstasie
Oriental Avenue	The Angel, Islington	Rathgar Road	West Street/ Weststraat
Vermont Avenue	Euston Road	South Circular Road	Smith Street/ Smithstraat
Connecticut Avenue	Pentonville Road	Rathmines Road	Marine Parade/ Marine Parade
St Charles Place	Pall Mall	Dawson Street	Monument Road/ Monumentweg
States Avenue	Whitehall	Merrion Street	Aliwal Street/ Aliwalstraat
Virginia Avenue	Northumberland Avenue	Nassau Street	Maitland Street/ Maitlandstraat
Pennsylvania Railroad	Marylebone Station	Dublin Airport	Bloemfontain Station/ Bloemfonteinstasie
St James Place	Bow Street	Pearse Street	President Brand Street/President Brandstraat
Tennessee Avenue	Marlborough Street	Dame Street	Hoffman Square/ Hoffmanplein
New York Avenue	Vine Street	Store Street	Voortrekker Road/ Voortrekkerweg
Kentucky Avenue	Strand	Oliver Plunket Street	Groote Schuur Street/ Groote Schuurstraat
Indiana Avenue	Fleet Street	Washington Street	Strand Street/ Strandstraat
Illinois Avenue	Trafalgar Square	Patrick Street	Roeland Street Roelandstraat
B. & C. Railroad	Fenchurch Street Station	Heuston Station	Cape Town Station/ Kaapstadstasie
Atlantic Avenue	Leicester Square	Talbot Street	Parliament Street/ Parliamentstraat

MONOPOLY AROUND THE WORLD
Boards used in English Speaking Countries

American	British	Irish	South African
Ventnor Avenue	Coventry Street	Earl Street	Plein Street/ Pleinstraat
Marvin Gardens	Piccadilly	O'Connell Street	Long Street/ Longstraat
Pacific Avenue	Regent Street	George's Street	Main Street/ Mainstraat
North Carolina Avenue	Oxford Street	Wicklow Street	Joubert Street/ Joubertstraat
Pennsylvania Avenue	Bond Street	Grafton Street	Devilliers Street/ Devilliersstraat
Short Line	Liverpool Street Station	Shannon Airport	Johannesburg Station/ Johannesburgstasie
Park Place	Park Lane	Ailesbury Road	Jan Smuts Avenue/ Jan Smutslaan
Boardwalk Road	Mayfair	Shrewsbury Road	Eloff Street/ Eloffstraat

The Australian Monopoly board.

MONOPOLY AROUND THE WORLD
Boards used in English Speaking Countries

Monopoly – The Facts

On his retirement in 1974, after 46 years with Waddingtons, sales representative Harry Bostel – the man who sold the first Monopoly game in the UK – was awarded a hand-made Monopoly set by the company. It cost £250 to produce and was presented in an inscribed teak case with special gold-plated tokens.

The Canadian Monopoly board.

THE ATLANTIC CITY AFFAIR

It is said that many American visitors to Atlantic City are surprised to find that the east coast resort has named all its streets after the streets on the American version of the Monopoly board: of course, the truth is that the American board has street names based on those of Atlantic City.

In September 1972 the city commissioners started a campaign to give Atlantic City a new image. This included a suggestion to change the names of Baltic Avenue and Mediterranean Avenue to Fairmont and Melrose. Baltic and Mediterranean Avenues are in the poorer part of the city, London's equivalent being Old Kent Road and Whitechapel Road. The proposal caused an uproar. Hundreds of letters, telegrams and phone calls from irate Monopoly players flooded into the city and into the offices of Parker Brothers. Protest organizations were formed, such as the SSBMA – 'Students to Save Baltic and Mediterranean Avenues'. The cause was taken up by newspapers and television.

The climax came in January 1973 at a public hearing in Atlantic City. Randolph P. Barton, executive vice-president of Parker Brothers, flew in to plead the cause, calling it, 'a disservice to both the game and the city to change these street names'. The president of Princeton's SSBMA said, 'The streets of Atlantic City, through the medium of Monopoly, have been a microcosm of life in which Baltic and Mediterranean have represented the last resort of the underdog to hold out against the oppressive forces of Boardwalk and Park Place powermongers.'

A letter to the commissioners from Edward J. Parker, president of Parker Brothers, also had its effect: 'Would you like to be the man to tell a Monopoly fanatic from California that the streets he came to see no longer exist? Would you be

THE ATLANTIC CITY
AFFAIR

willing to take the responsibility for an invasion by hordes of protesting Monopoly players, all demanding that you go directly to Jail, without even the dignity of passing GO?'

The five-man commission unanimously agreed to veto the proposal.

Monopoly – The Facts

Short Line is one of the railroads on the American board – but it is not, and never has been, a railroad. When Charles Darrow was thinking up the game he ran out of railroads and included Short Line as the next best thing. At the time it was the name of a freight-carrying bus company with a depot in Atlantic City. Short Line is still an active New York bus line which specializes in luxury motor coach tours

CRIMINAL CONNECTIONS

The Great Train Robbers of 1963 were found to have played Monopoly when detectives discovered their fingerprints on a board at their Leatherslade hide-out in Cheddington, Bucks.

Back in the mid-seventies something of a furore was created when several long-sentence prisoners in Britain's top-security prisons were refused permission to play the game. It led to a formal complaint to the Ombudsman.

In 1980 there was the case of the woman who tried to board a Colombia-bound plane carrying the six sets of Monopoly. Treasury agents became suspicious and when they ordered her to open the boxes they found that each contained $250 000 in real money. She was detained for violating the US law which requires that the movement of $5000 or more in cash be reported to the government, but the authorities' real suspicion was that the hoard was a drugs pay-off.

TYCOON MONOPOLY

One of the most sensational games of Monopoly ever played took place in Brown's Hotel in London in 1970. The players were six of the country's leading financiers and personalities and the game was televized on the BBC's *Money Programme*.

The players were: Jim Slater* of Slater Walker fame; Nigel Broackes of Trafalgar House; Oliver Jessel of Jessel Securities; David Malbert, City Editor of the London Evening News; Robert Morley, actor, gambler and eccentric; and Sir John Cohen, president and founder of the Tesco supermarket group. Victor Watson, Managing Director of Waddingtons, acted as adjudicator.

The early play was fast and exciting as each player tried to build up a dominating position on the board. Not doing at all badly for a tycoon who had played only three times before, Sir John began to build up strategic locations such as Mayfair, Park Lane, Northumberland Avenue, Whitechapel Road and Pall Mall. Jim Slater got off to a bad start by landing on Income Tax and having to pay £200. However, after some tough bargaining with Robert Morley and Nigel Broackes, he was able to add Vine Street and Bow Street to Marlborough Street, giving him the complete orange property group. Robert Morley sold Bond Street to Oliver Jessel for the extortionate sum of £1000, and began building hotels on Pentonville Road, Euston Road and The Angel, Islington. This led to him maintaining a strong position throughout the game.

The inevitable was not long in coming. In the fortieth minute, Nigel Broackes' dice landed him in serious trouble,

---

* Jim Slater was later to publish an account of the rise and fall of his financial empire, under the title *Return To Go*.

TYCOON MONOPOLY

and he had to sell three houses on the yellow property group to pay £550 to Jim Slater. Soon after, Oliver Jessel followed suit and had to mortgage two stations in order to pay Jim the rent for landing on Marlborough Street. He also threw in Whitechapel Road as part of the bargain.

Bargaining continued between the players. Jim Slater, who began having cash flow problems, offered Whitechapel and Old Kent Road to Robert Morley for £450, then for £425, and then for £400. The offer was not accepted.

David Malbert had to pay £850 to Nigel Broackes when he landed on Piccadilly with three houses. This signalled the beginning of the end of his brief business career. In quick succession Nigel Broackes and Robert Morley landed on Mayfair, and Sir John Cohen collected £1400 rent from each of them. Nigel Broackes was out of luck, for soon afterwards he landed on Morley's The Angel, Islington and, unable to pay the rent of £550, he had to quit the game.

Sir John's strategic planning was beginning to pay off handsomely, as he continued erecting more houses throughout his property empire. Oliver Jessel went bankrupt after landing on Mayfair. A few minutes later Jim Slater went the same way.

Sir John now had only Robert Morley to beat. When, after landing on Park Lane, Morley's assets were insufficient to

Monopoly – The Facts

The most expensive Monopoly set ever made was manufactured by Alfred Dunhill, and retailed for $5000

TYCOON MONOPOLY

pay the rent, Sir John emerged victorious.

Lighting a cigar with a £500 note, Sir John remarked, 'This is only the fourth time I have played Monopoly in my life. I don't think I shall ever be so lucky again.'

Monopoly – The Facts

A braille edition of Monopoly is available through the American Foundation for the Blind, 15 West 16th Street, New York, NY 10011, USA

COMPUTER MONOPOLY

It is not only humans who play Monopoly – now computers also play the game. Under licence from Parker Brothers and Waddingtons, Leisure Genius have devised a computer version of Monopoly for the Commodore 64 home micro.

2 to 6 players can participate and the computer, as well as acting as Banker, can also act as any or all of the players!

The computer, as Banker and as player, is of course scrupulously fair – and it never makes mistakes. Nevertheless it is not as adaptable as a human player – it can't vary its style of play depending on the opponents it meets. So a human, particularly one who has learnt from the tips in this book, should stand a reasonable chance against the electronic brain.

Other computer software has also been prepared recently – versions for the Spectrum and the Amstrad were released in the spring and summer of 1985.

Monopoly – The Facts

In 1978, Neiman-Marcus Stores of Dallas, USA, offered a $600 chocolate Monopoly set for sale in its Christmas catalogue

THE MONOPOLY QUIZ
TEST YOUR KNOWLEDGE
OF THE GAME
The Questions

Here are twenty questions to test your knowledge of
Monopoly. See how many questions you can answer and
then check your score to see how good a player you are.

1 How much cash does each player have to start the
   game?

2 Suppose you own all four Railway Stations but you have
   mortgaged two of them. Your opponent lands on one of
   the Railway Stations you have *not* mortgaged. How
   much rent do you collect?

3 Which of the three sites in the red property group is
   landed on most often – Strand, Fleet Street or Trafalgar
   Square?

4 Can you describe two situations in which you do *not* get
   another throw of the dice after throwing doubles?

5 What is the rent for Mayfair with a hotel on it?

6 A player who is in Jail can not bid for property that is
   sold by auction. Is this true or false?

7 Is there any situation in which you are allowed to buy
   houses from another player?

8 If you mortgage The Angel, Islington you receive £50
   from the Bank. How much do you have to pay the Bank
   when you lift the mortgage?

9 If you pay the £50 fine to get out of Jail and then throw doubles, you get your £50 back because throwing doubles gets you out of Jail free. Is this true or false?

10 At the beginning of the game how many houses does the Bank have available to sell?

11 Which of the four Railway Stations is landed on least frequently?

12 If you land on a property owned by another player and he does not ask for the rent until after the next player has thrown the dice, you do not need to pay. Is this true or false?

13 Which of the two Utilities is landed on most frequently?

14 How many players may be in Jail at the same time?

15 You are not allowed to transfer mortgaged property to another player – you must lift the mortgage first. Is this true or false?

16 When you throw the two dice, what is the probability that they will show a total value of 9?

17 Can you sell mortgaged property back to the Bank if you do not have enough cash to pay fines or taxes?

18 If you own two complete property groups the best strategy is to erect three houses on each property of one

group before you start erecting any houses on the other group of properties. Is this true or false?

19 It will normally cost you £150 to buy a house to erect on Piccadilly. Is there any situation where you could possibly buy a house for Piccadilly for less than £150?

20 When you advance your token to Mayfair as a result of drawing the Chance card which says 'Advance to Mayfair', are you entitled to £200 salary if you pass GO? (Think carefully)

THE MONOPOLY QUIZ
The Answers

1 £1500.

2 £50.

3 Trafalgar Square.

4 (a) When you have thrown doubles with three consecutive throws of the dice.
   (b) When you land on GO TO JAIL as a result of throwing a double.
   (c) If you pick a Chance or Community Chest card sending you to Jail.

5 £2000.

6 False. (Unless you are playing the Maximum Penalty version of the game.) In the standard version of the game a player who is in Jail can still buy and sell property or buildings, mortgage property, trade, and collect rents.

7 No. Houses may only be bought from the Bank.

8 £55 – that is the mortgage value (£50) plus 10 per cent interest (£5).

9 False.

10 32.

11 Liverpool Street.

THE MONOPOLY QUIZ
The Answers

12 True.

13 Water Works.

14 Any number.

15 False. (Mortgaged property may be transferred from one player to another with the proviso that the player who receives it must either lift the mortgage immediately or pay 10 per cent interest on the mortgage value.)

16 The probability is 4/36 (or 1/9, which is the same thing). This means that *on average* the dice will show a total value of 9 once in every nine throws.

17 No. (There is no provision in the rules for the Bank to buy back any property, whether it is mortgaged or not. Only buildings may be sold back to the Bank.)

18 True.

19 Yes. When there is a building shortage and the Bank sells houses by auction.

20 This was a trick question. If you look at the board, you will see that it is impossible to pass GO when you advance your token to Mayfair.

THE MONOPOLY QUIZ
How Did You Score?

If you scored over 20	You can't count.
If you scored 18–20	You must be a top-rate Monopoly player. Have you thought about entering for the World Monopoly Championship?
If you scored 14–17	You are a good player, but you need to read this book once more to sharpen up your game.
If you scored 10–13	You still have a lot to learn about Monopoly. Buy five more copies of the book.
If you scored less than 10	Go directly to Jail. Do not pass GO. Do not collect £200.

The Complacent Player's Warning

If you're confident of winning every game it may be because you don't know enough to know better

Appendix

OFFICIAL MONOPOLY
RULES

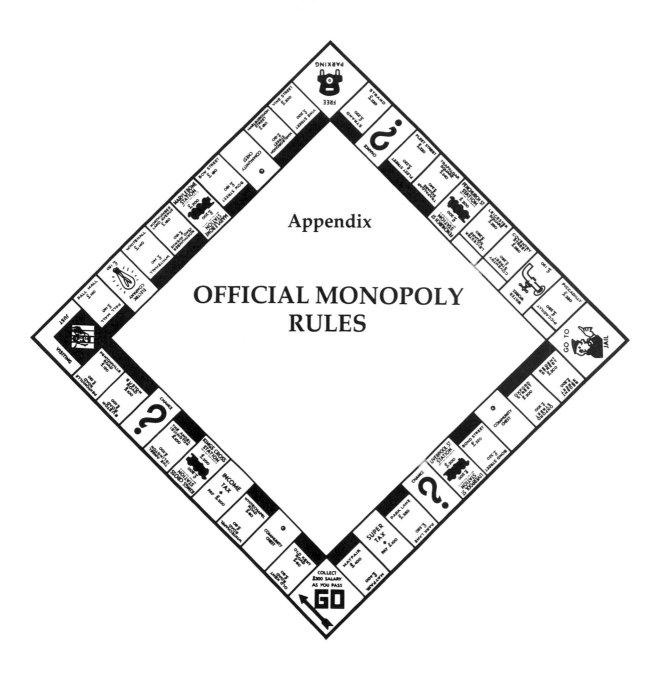

OFFICIAL MONOPOLY RULES

The Law of the Land

Ignorance is no excuse

The Monopoly Corollary

Now you've got the book, play by the rules

Brief Idea of the Game

The idea of the game is to buy and rent or sell properties so profitably that players increase their wealth – the wealthiest becoming the eventual winner. Starting from 'GO', move the tokens around the board according to throw of the dice. When a player's token lands on a space not already owned, he may buy it from the Bank: otherwise it is auctioned off to the highest bidder. The object of owning property is to collect rents from opponents stopping there. Rentals are greatly increased by the erection of Houses and Hotels, so it is wise to build them on some of your Building Sites. To raise more money, Building Sites may be mortgaged to the Bank. Community Chest and Chance cards give instructions that must be followed. Sometimes players land in Jail. The game is one of shrewd and amusing trading and excitement.

OFFICIAL MONOPOLY RULES

Equipment

Monopoly Real Estate Trading Game Equipment consists of the board with spaces indicating Building Sites, Railway Stations, Utilities, rewards and penalties over which the player's pieces are moved. There are two dice, tokens of various designs for playing pieces, thirty-two green Houses, twelve red Hotels and two sets of cards for Chance and Community Chest spaces. There are Title Deed cards for every property and 'bank notes' of various denominations.

Preparation

Place the board on a good-sized table, putting the Chance cards and Community Chest cards face down on their allotted spaces on the board. Each player is provided with one token to represent him on his travels around the board. Each player is given £1500. All other equipment goes to the Bank. One of the players is elected Banker. (See *Bank* and *Banker*.)

Money

Each player is given £1500 divided as follows: two £500 – four £100 – one £50 – one £20 – two £10 – one £5 – five £1's.

All remaining money goes to the Bank.

OFFICIAL MONOPOLY RULES

To Start the Game

Starting with the Banker, each player in turn throws the dice.
The player with the highest total starts the play. He places
his token on the corner marked 'GO', throws the dice and
moves his token in the direction of the Arrow the number of
spaces indicated by the dice. After he has completed his
play, the turn to play passes to the left. The tokens remain on
the spaces occupied and proceed from that point on the
player's next turn. One or more tokens may rest on the same
space at the same time.

According to the space which his token reaches, a player
may be entitled to buy Building Sites or other properties – or
be obliged to pay rent (if another owns the property), pay
taxes, draw a Chance or Community Chest card, 'Go to Jail',
etc.

If a player throws doubles he moves his token as usual, the
sum of the two dice, and the space thus reached is effective
(i.e. the player is subject to any privileges or penalties
pertaining to that space). Retaining the dice, he throws again
and moves his token as before, and again, the space thus
reached is effective. If, however, he throws three doubles in
succession, he does not move his token on his third throw
but immediately 'goes to jail', and his turn ends. (See *Jail*.)

Every time that a player's token either lands on or passes
over 'GO', while going in the direction of the Arrow, the
Banker pays him £200 'Salary'.

OFFICIAL MONOPOLY RULES

Landing on Unowned Property

When a player lands on an unowned property (i.e. on a Building Site for which no other player holds the Title Deed) whether by a throw of the dice or by a move forced by the draw of a Chance or Community Chest card, the player has the option of buying that property from the Bank at its printed price. If a player elects to buy, he pays the Bank for that property and receives the Title Deed card showing ownership which he places face-up in front of him. If the player declines his option, the Banker must immediately offer this property for sale by auction and must sell it to the highest bidder, accepting money in payment and give the buyer the proper Title Deed card as evidence of ownership. Any player, including the one who declined the option of buying at the printed price, may bid. Bidding may start at any price.

Landing on Owned Property

When a player lands on owned property either by throw of dice, or by a move forced by a Chance or Community Chest card, the owner collects rent from him in accordance with the list printed on the Title Deed card applying to it. Note: if the Site contains a House or Houses, the rent is larger than it would be for an unimproved Site. If the Site is mortgaged, no rent can be collected. Double rent cannot be collected from a Colour-Group if one Site is mortgaged. A player holding four Stations, but with one mortgaged, may only collect rent from the other three – i.e. he would collect £100 – not £200. Mortgaged property is designated by turning face-down the Title Deed representing that property.

Note: if the owner fails to ask for his rent before the next throw of the dice no rent may be collected.

OFFICIAL MONOPOLY RULES

Advantages for Owners

It is an advantage to hold Title Deeds for all Sites of a complete Colour-Group (for example: Mayfair and Park Lane – or Pentonville Road, Euston Road and The Angel, Islington) because the owner may then charge double rent for unimproved Sites of that property. (See 'Title Deed' cards.)

Houses can only be built on Sites of a complete Colour-Group owned (see *Houses*).

The advantage of owning Houses and Hotels rather than unimproved property is that rentals are very much higher than for unimproved Sites and profit the owner immensely.

OFFICIAL MONOPOLY RULES

Landing on 'Chance' or 'Community Chest'

A player takes the top card from the pack indicated and after following the instructions printed thereon, returns the card face down to the bottom of the pack. The 'Get out of Jail free' card, however, is retained until used. After being used, it is returned to the bottom of the pack. This card may be sold by a player to another player at a price agreeable to both.

Landing on Tax Spaces

Pay all taxes to the Bank.

Landing on 'Free Parking'

When, in the ordinary course of play, a player's token reaches this space, the player receives no benefit nor incurs any penalty, and moves ahead in the usual manner on his next turn.

OFFICIAL MONOPOLY RULES

Banker

Select as Banker a player who will also make a good auctioneer. If, as is customary, the Banker also plays in the game, he must, of course, keep his personal funds separate from those of the Bank. When more than five persons play, the Banker sometimes elects to act only as Banker and Auctioneer.

The Bank

The Banker preferably uses for the Bank a small side-table placed at his elbow and the game box, or a good-sized container. The Bank holds, besides the Bank's money, the Title Deed cards and Houses and Hotels prior to purchase and use by the players.

The Bank pay salaries and bonuses, sells properties to the players and delivers the proper Title Deed cards therefor, auctions Sites, sells Houses and Hotels to the players, loans money when required on mortgages of property at the mortgage value which is one-half of the Site value printed on the board. The Bank will at any time buy back Houses and Hotels from Building Sites at half price.

If the Bank runs out of money the Banker must issue IOU's for whatever amounts are required. (They can be made out on any small pieces of paper available, simply write IOU and then the required amount.) These can be exchanged for cash whenever cash is available, otherwise they are simply counted in the assets of the player holding them.

Pay to the Bank the price of all properties you buy from it, taxes, fines, money penalties, loans and interest.

Jail

A player lands in Jail – (1) If his token lands on the space marked 'GO TO JAIL'. (2) If he draws a card marked 'GO TO JAIL'. (3) If he throws doubles three times in succession.

Note: When a player is sent to Jail his turn ends there. He cannot collect £200 Salary in that move since, regardless of where his token is or of the path of the board, he must move his token directly into Jail.

Visiting Jail. If a player is not 'sent to Jail' but in the ordinary course of play reaches that space, he is 'just visiting', incurs no penalty, and moves ahead in the usual manner on his next turn.

A player gets out of Jail – (1) By throwing doubles on any of his next three turns after landing in Jail. If he succeeds in doing this he immediately moves forward the number of spaces shown by his doubles throw; he also has another throw of the dice. (2) Purchasing a 'Get out of Jail free' card from another player, at a price agreeable to both (unless he already owns such a card by having on a previous turn drawn it from Chance or Community Chest). (3) By paying a £50 fine before he throws the dice for either his next or succeeding turn to play. (4) A player must not remain in Jail after his third turn (i.e. not longer than having three turns to play after being sent to Jail). Immediately after throwing the dice for his third turn he must pay a £50 fine unless he throws doubles. He then comes out and immediately moves forward from Jail the number of spaces shown by his throw.

A player may buy or erect a House, sell or buy property, and collect rentals, even though he is in Jail.

OFFICIAL MONOPOLY RULES

Houses

Houses can be bought only from the Bank and can only be erected on Sites of a complete Colour-Group which the player owns. (Example: If one player succeeds in owning Pentonville Road, Euston Road and The Angel, Islington, i.e. a complete Colour-Group, he may at any period of his ownership buy a House or Houses from the Bank to erect thereon. If he buys one House, he may put it on any one of these three Sites. The next House he buys and erects must be put on one of the unoccupied Sites of this or of any other complete Colour-Group he may own. The price he must pay the Bank for each House is shown on his Title Deed of the Site. (On the unimproved Sites of his complete Colour-Group he continues collecting double rental from an opponent landing thereon.)

A player may buy and erect in accordance with the above rules, at any time, except during an opponent's turn, as many Houses or Hotels as his judgment and financial standing will allow, but he must build evenly. He cannot erect more than one House on any one Site of any Colour-Group until he has built one House on every Site of that Group. He may then begin on the second row of Houses and so on up to limit of four Houses to a Site. He cannot build, for example, three Houses on one Site if he has only one House on another Site of that Group. Similarly, Sites must be maintained evenly – i.e. if Houses have to be sold they must be removed equally from Sites of a Colour-Group. Houses may not be built on Sites if one of the same Colour-Group is mortgaged.

OFFICIAL MONOPOLY RULES

Hotels

A player must have four Houses on each Site of a complete Colour-Group before he can buy an Hotel. He may then buy an Hotel from the Bank to be erected on any site of that Colour-Group, delivering to the Bank in payment, the four Houses already on the Site plus the additional cost of the Hotel (£200 for an Hotel on Park Lane or Mayfair) shown on the Title Deed. (It is very desirable to erect Hotels on account of the very large rental which may be charged. Only one Hotel may be erected on any one Site.)

Building Shortage

When the Bank has no Houses to sell, players wishing to build must wait for some player to return or to sell his Houses to the Bank before they can build. If there are a limited number of Houses and Hotels available, and two or more players wish to buy more than the Bank has, the Houses or Hotels must be sold by auction to the highest bidder.

OFFICIAL MONOPOLY RULES

Selling Property

Undeveloped Sites, Railway Stations and Utilities (but not buildings thereon) may be sold to any player as a private transaction for any amount that the owner can get. No Site, however, can be sold to another player if buildings are standing on any Sites of that Colour-Group. Any buildings so situated must be sold back to the Bank before the owner can sell any Site of that Colour-Group. Mortgaged property cannot be sold to the Bank – only to other players.

Houses and Hotels may be resold by players to the Bank only, but this may be done at any time and the Bank will pay one half of the price paid for them. In the case of Hotels, the Bank will pay half the cash price of the Hotel plus half the price of the four Houses which were given in the purchase of the Hotel.

OFFICIAL MONOPOLY RULES

Mortgages

Mortgaging properties can be done through the Bank only. The mortgage value is printed on each Title Deed. The rate of interest is 10 per cent, payable when the mortgage is lifted. If any property is transferred which is mortgaged, the new owner may lift the mortgage at once if he wishes, but he must pay 10 per cent interest. If he fails to lift the mortgage, he still pays 10 per cent interest and if he lifts the mortgage later he pays an additional 10 per cent interest as well as the principal.

Houses or Hotels cannot be mortgaged. All buildings on the Site must be sold back to the Bank before any property can be mortgaged. The Bank will only pay one half of what was paid for them.

In order to rebuild a House on mortgaged property the owner must pay the Bank the amount of the mortgage, plus the 10 per cent interest charge and buy the House back from the Bank at its full price.

OFFICIAL MONOPOLY RULES

Bankruptcy

A player who is bankrupt, that is, one who owes more than he can pay, must turn over to his creditor all that he has of value, and retire from the game. In making this settlement, however, if he owns Houses or Hotels, these are returned to the Bank in exchange for money, to the extent of half their cost as printed on the Title Deeds, and this cash is given to the creditor. If a bankrupt player turns over to his creditor property that has been mortgaged, the new owner must at once pay the Bank the 10 per cent interest on the loan. At the same time he may at his option lift the mortgage by paying the principal.

In case a player is unable to raise money enough to pay his taxes or penalties, even by selling his buildings and mortgaging his property, the Bank will take over all his assets and sell by auction to the highest bidder everything so taken except the buildings. The player must then remove his token. The last player left in the game wins.

Miscellaneous

If a player owes more rent than he can pay in cash he may pay his creditor part in cash and part in property. In this case, the creditor will often accept certain property (even if it is mortgaged) at a value far in excess of the printed one so as to obtain additional property for buildings or to block another player from obtaining control of that property.

Property owners must watch out for rents due. Do not help other players to watch their properties.

The Bank loans money only on mortgage security. Players may not borrow money or property from each other.

OFFICIAL MONOPOLY RULES

Rules for Playing the Short Game

Before commencing, the players stipulate the time at which the game shall end. At the end of the game the richest player is the winner.

At the start of the game the Banker shuffles the Title Deed cards and, after having cut them, he deals two cards to each player. The players immediately pay to the Bank the price of the property thus dealt to them.

The game then proceeds in the usual manner until the agreed finishing time is reached. No further dealings must take place, but if a player is in actual play when the finish is announced, he is allowed to complete his move, and any transactions in connection with it. Each player then totals up the value of his possessions: (1) Cash in hand. (2) Building Sites, Utilities or Railway Stations owned by him, at the price printed on the board. (3) Mortgaged property at half the price printed on the board. (4) Houses owned valued at their respective cost prices. (5) Hotels, valued at the cost of five houses.

The player with the highest total is the winner.

OFFICIAL MONOPOLY RULES

Brandreth's Last Word

Never forget: it's only a game